D0699374

The Labour Party
and the Working Class

TOM FORESTER

The Labour Party and the Working Class

HEINEMANN
London

Heinemann Educational Books Ltd
LONDON EDINBURGH MELBOURNE AUCKLAND TORONTO
HONG KONG SINGAPORE KUALA LUMPUR
IBADAN NAIROBI JOHANNESBURG
LUSAKA NEW DELHI

ISBN 0 435 82309 4

Published by
Heinemann Educational Books Ltd
48 Charles Street, London W1X 8AH
Printed in Great Britain at
The Pitman Press, Bath

Contents

Preface

Most people, especially the leftward-thinking, have puzzled about the problem of the Labour Party at some time in their intellectual development. This book treats the Labour Party as a problem-area, and is written for them – constituency activists, trade unionists, individual socialists, university and college students. It is written in the hope that it will help others understand the Labour Party better, as it did me in the course of writing it. At the same time, it represents an attempt to communicate some of the existing knowledge accumulated by academic social science to a wider public.

By its very nature the book is both a 'popular' text, and a general 'review' of other books, articles and research and, as publishers like to say, it is aimed at the 'general reader'.

Of course, combining a popular approach with a general review brings its own problems, problems about which I am now only too fully aware. In consequence I have not always been as critical as I would have liked of some authors, some problems have not been fully explored, and many questions remain unanswered.

My aim throughout has been to provide a general introductory text for people unfamiliar with – or unable to obtain – the relevant literature. A selected bibliography is provided for those readers who wish to follow up particular lines of enquiry themselves, and Appendix A essentially provides an account of how to conduct a social survey.

For help in connection with the Constituency Labour Party survey, I would like in particular to thank Bob Brown, Nobby Clarke and Jennifer Platt for their assistance, Tony Howard for his encouragement, and Alan Marsh for an enormous amount of help with the questionnaire and analysis of the data. Indeed, without Alan's assistance the survey would not have been possible. Finally, I would like to thank Tom Bottomore, Jim Sharpe and Stephen Yeo for their helpful advice and comments.

Tom Forester,
December 1975.

Introduction

Chapter One contains introductory material setting out two broad aims of the book – to examine the relationship between the Labour Party and the working class and to throw some light on the experience of social democracy in Britain. The history of the British Labour Party is placed within the context of the achievements and failings of Western European social democracy.

In Chapter Two, I am primarily concerned with the facts concerning the British class structure and the electoral relationship between the Labour Party and the working class. Do most of the working class vote Labour? Who else votes Labour? Why do one third of the working class not vote Labour? Is the electoral allegiance of the working class to the Labour Party being eroded? Starting from a survey of the electoral facts, and a discussion of the reasons put forward to explain these facts, I will go on to examine two theories involving the alleged 'de-radicalization' of both the Labour Party and its working class electorate. Each can be seen as an attempt to identify imminent change in the electoral stalemate of social democracy.

The first of these is the 'affluent worker' or 'embourgeoisement' thesis, which will be considered briefly. The second – the 'decline of working class politics' theses – will be treated at greater length because I believe that it raises important questions about class consciousness and the historical role of the Labour Party. In addition, an examination of this argument necessarily involves an appraisal of the historical and contemporary evidence concerning the operation of, and working class participation in, the Labour Party at the local level.

In Chapter Three, therefore, the discussion of these theories leads into a general analysis of the Labour Party, and in this I have attempted to isolate key problems of general interest and points relevant to the preceding discussion. In particular, if a 'decline of working class politics' is alleged, if a 'de-radicalization' of social democratic parties is implied, then one must be able to clearly identify what they have 'declined' or 'de-radicalized' from. In order to argue, say, that the Labour Party is 'no longer socialist', one must be able to explain in what senses it was more 'socialist' in the past than it is now. The sort of questions we will be asking include: *Is* the Labour Party socialist? Was the Labour Party *ever* socialist? In what senses? Has socialism been betrayed by the Labour Party? Or forgotten? These are problems of historical interpretation, and we must attempt to answer them with reference to the very origins of the Labour Party, the kind of society that gave birth to it, and the subsequent social changes which have moulded and largely determined the Labour Party we know today.

The significance of all this should not be underestimated. Different interpretations of the history of the Labour Party have led to very different analyses of what the Labour Party 'really' is, and this in turn often hinges on the kind of relationship the party is alleged to have, or has had, with the working class. For many people basically sympathetic to Labour, their perceived history of the Labour Party is crucial in determining their attitude to the party, and hence their own political practice – whether to work for the Labour Party, merely to vote for it, or simply to ignore it. For active socialists, it is a decision about whether to 'accept' and work wholeheartedly for it, 'reject' and perhaps work against it, or reach an ambivalent accommodation with it midway between acceptance and rejection. For example, there are essentially two polar types of history of the Labour Party, which might be called the 'History of the Glorious Struggle', and the 'History of Betrayal'. Persons who accept the latter analysis are hardly likely to dedicate their life to working for the Labour Party, though some might work within it.

One way to illuminate a broader question is to focus on a particularly instructive part which can provide insights of relevance to the whole. In Chapter Four I concentrate on Constituency Labour Parties and their role in the local community, drawing on both historical and contemporary evidence. This is a sadly neglected area of study. There are plenty of histories of the Labour Party which concentrate on dramatic events in the history of the Parliamentary Labour Party, and there are numerous biographies of Labour leaders, but very little is known about the kind of people who built the local party organizations in the past and sustain them today. Some would say that this is because there is very little to be known or very little worth knowing, but I believe the evidence we do have concerning the operation of the Labour Party at the local level can do much to help us to understand the more general problems of the Labour Party.

Moreover, changes occuring in the grass roots could have important consequences for the party at the national level. For instance, Barry Hindess, the author most closely associated with the 'decline of working class politics' thesis, has argued this.[1]

Other writers and commentators too, have argued, like Hindess, that the local organizations of the Labour Party are collapsing or are being taken over by the middle classes. If this is true, then obviously it would have important consequences for an ostensibly mass party 'of' and 'for' the working class.

Chapter Five contains some original material from a study of one Constituency Labour Party, Brighton Kemptown. Most of the evidence is drawn from a questionnaire survey of every member of Kemptown CLP which was conducted in 1973, and Chapter Five mainly consists of a fairly detailed analysis of data generated from the questionnaire. An account of how the survey was carried out is presented in Appendix A at the end of the book. Suffice it to say here that the research was specifically designed to examine some aspects of the 'de-radicalization' and 'decline of working class politics' theories.

In Chapter Six, I make further comment of the arguments and evidence cited in the preceding chapters, and attempt to draw out some relevant conclusions.

---

[1] Hindess, B., *The Decline of Working Class Politics*, MacGibbon & Kee, 1971.

1. The Labour Party Seventy-five Years On

Seventy-five years of the Labour Party have not brought socialism. Nobody would deny that, but we have to ask the question why, and this book, in part, is an attempt to help answer it. Most of the delegates who assembled to form the Labour Representation Committee in the Memorial Hall, Farringdon Street, London, on 27 February 1900 had extremely modest aims. But by 1918 committed socialists within the early Labour Party did succeed in converting a pressure group primarily concerned with increasing Labour representation into a political party explicitly dedicated to transforming society through the ballot box. One aim of the Party was to be, as Clause IV of the Constitution adopted in 1918 would have it:

> To secure for the workers by hand or by brain the full fruits of their industry and the most equitable distribution thereof that may be possible, upon the basis of the common ownership of the means of production and the best obtainable system of popular administration and control of each industry and service.

If this accurately represented the hopes and desires of the early pioneers, then their hopes have not been fulfilled. Just as the formation of an explicitly socialist party did not automatically lead to socialism when that party finally achieved a lengthy period of parliamentary power, so neither did the creation of the universal franchise automatically mean that the party with most working class support would have a permanent parliamentary majority. Marx was not the only one who got this wrong when he wrote in 1852 that:

> ... Universal suffrage is the equivalent of political power for the working class of England, where the proletariat forms the large majority of the population ... The carrying of universal suffrage in England would, therefore, be a far more socialist measure than anything which

has been honoured with that name on the Continent. Its inevitable result here, is the *political supremacy of the working class*.[1]

This statement is either right in that the working class are already politically supreme by Marx's definition because they form the majority of the population, and everybody has the vote – or it is wrong, as is surely the case, in that the working class have not yet in any real sense become 'politically supreme'. Of course the logical fallacy is to assume that the 'working class' is a unified political whole because in reality it consists of different individuals, approximately one third of whom do not even give electoral support to the Party which was originally and specifically founded to represent working class interests. The Labour Party did not, and has still not, secured the electoral allegiance of more than about two-thirds of the working class, and to throw some light on this phenomenon is one reason why I want to focus on the relationship between Labour and the working class.

A secondary reason reflects broader concerns. From the time when Marx was engaged on his analysis of nineteenth-century capitalism to the present day, there have been a number of political options open to working class people anxious to improve their standard of life. These have included, first, the revolutionary movement under the leadership of a revolutionary party, aiming to overthrow capitalism by smashing the state machine through mass action; second, the extension of worker's control or syndicalism through factory occupations and other industrial action; third, the reformist mass party, with or without close Trade Union links, aiming at a socialist parliamentary majority, and based on the electoral support of the overwhelming numbers of working class voters; finally, one might add the option of political apathy or quiescence. This implies that the best political course open to working class people is to sit back and enjoy the fruits of imperialism, neo-colonialism, or whatever, leaving political statesmanship and decision-making in the first instance to those who are born to rule, and in the second, to those who can run Great Britain Limited most efficiently. It has been suggested that this approach is favoured by the 'working class Tories', and it differs from the other three in that it doesn't offer any kind of alternative to capitalism, while the other three options do. Here, I am wholly concerned with an example of the third strategy – the reformist mass party or social democratic party, which has historically been a major type of working class party under Western capitalism.

Now political democracy itself is very much a twentieth century

---

[1] Marx, K., 'The Chartists', *New York Daily Tribune*, 25 Aug. 1852.

phenomenon. It is chiefly characterized by the existence of a universal franchise, certain political freedoms, and the apparent representation of different social interests through the medium of political parties. Social democracy, on the other hand, is a term generally used to refer to those political democracies, especially Western European ones, where a predominantly private enterprise economic system exists, but where some degree of state intervention in the economy and state provision of welfare services is accepted as the norm by all the major political parties. More often than not, the term social democracy is also used with reference to the Socialist, Social Democratic and Labour Parties which exist in many Western countries with the express intention of changing the 'reward structure' of those societies, i.e. the distribution of wealth, income, opportunity and privilege. Labour Parties can be seen as a particular form of social democratic party, distinguishable mainly by their close links with Trade Unions.[2]

Another purpose of this book is, therefore, to throw some light on the workings and experience of social democracy in one Western European country, Britain. With the British Labour Party now three-quarters of a century old, this may be an opportune time to do so. Since the Labour Party, like other social democratic parties, grew rapidly along with the newly enfranchised working class electorate, an understanding of the social democratic experience in Britain calls for a re-examination of the relationship between the Labour Party and the working class; and because the apparent stability of party politics in Britain rests largely on the continued electoral allegiance to the Labour Party of nearly two-thirds of the working class, a greater understanding of this key relationship will not only help us to understand what social democracy and present-day society is all about, it may also give us valuable insights into the kind of political change, or lack of change, which we might expect to see in the future – for a change in this key relationship may have wider repercussions. Of course, any diagnosis of the future must begin in the past as well as the present, so much of the book will be drawing on both historical and contemporary evidence concerning Labour and the working class.

The European Social Democratic Experience

In his book *Class Inequality and Political Order*, Frank Parkin began by asking, quite simply, what have the working class political parties

---

[2] For an interesting though ultimately inconsequential analysis of the world's Labour parties, see Rawson, D. W., 'The Life-Span of Labour Parties', *Political Studies*, 1969 vol XVII, no 3.

achieved? And in what way does their socialist ideology at present constitute a challenge to the reward-structure of modern capitalism? He
suggested that the best way to tackle the first question was to compare the
state of play in those Western countries which have had social democratic
governments for long periods (e.g. Norway, Sweden), with those which
have not (e.g. Britain, France), to see if the different government ideologies
would explain variations in the social structure of each country.[3] Three key
social indicators were selected – rates of social mobility, educational opportunity, and the distribution of wealth. He then compared the performance of each country on each criterion and concluded, in the case of social
mobility, that '. . . the evidence would seem to favour those who wished to
show some connection between political ideology and social
stratification',[4] i.e. in countries where social democratic governments had
been in power, greater opportunities existed for the individual to move upward (or downward) through the class structure. For educational opportunity, he also concluded that though variations between all countries were
not great, there was definitely some evidence, especially from Scandinavia,
to suggest that the socialist ideals of successive social democratic
governments had made some progressive impact on the educational
system. On the distribution of wealth he was less optimistic, and concluded
that social democratic administrations, even in Scandinavia, do not seem
to have checked 'the drive towards inequality, inherent in a market
system'.[5]

This failing on Parkin's third criterion is crucial because it implies that
'socialist' governments in capitalist countries have not been able to overcome the pressures of the market and 'where income narrowing has occurred, this has been due more to long-run social and industrial trends than
to the effect of egalitarian ideologies'.[6] While progress in the form of
greater social mobility between classes or in greater educational opportunity may be worthy in themselves, they are still only to do with giving less
privileged people a better chance of 'getting on'. It doesn't necessarily
mean that there exists a more general move towards equality. 'In other
words', Parkin concludes, 'Social Democrats appear to have been more

---

[3] Parkin, F., *Class Inequality and Political Order*, MacGibbon & Kee, 1971.

[4] *ibid.*, p. 109.

[5] *ibid.*, p. 121. John Strachey, for example, also argued in 1956 that '. . . Capitalism has, in fact, an in-
nate tendency to extreme and ever-growing inequality. For how otherwise could all the culminatively
equalitarian measures, which the popular forces have succeeded in enacting over the last hundred years,
done little more than hold the position constant?' Strachey, J., *Contemporary Capitalism*, Gollancz,
1956, pp. 150–1.

[6] Parkin, *op. cit.*, p. 121.

able or willing to broaden the social base of recruitment to privileged positions than to equalize rewards attached to different positions.'[7] This, says Parkin, is therefore a 'meritocratic' version of socialism rather than traditional 'egalitarian' socialism. It is really based on 'fairness' in competition for privileges, with rewards being determined by the market, not by human needs. As two further thoughts, he adds that this kind of 'meritocratic' socialism practised by the Social Democrats in Western Europe may in fact lead to the more efficient operation of capitalism, in that it allows 'talented' people to rise to the top more easily – and by this definition of socialism, the United States, for instance, could conceivably be considered 'socialist' already.

Anderson, too, has argued that an international comparison would reveal no correlation between the existence of social democratic governments and the percentage of industry under public ownership, or with the most redistributive tax systems, or with the level of state provision of welfare services.[8] He suggested that social democracy has not only not brought about socialism, it has failed to affect *any* major structural changes in Western European societies.

The reason for this is that social democracy has been too easily absorbed by 'the encircling pressures of Capitalist Society'.[9] The great gulf between the aims and actual effect of social democratic parties results primarily from their failure to understand the nature of power. Power, he says, does not simply consist of a legislative majority or control of the 'means of legislation', but in reality has other bases, like the ownership of capital or the 'means of production'. In fact, 'power' is not an 'object' at all, but is intimately bound-up with the many kinds of relationships involving power, which constitute a capitalist society. Unless these relationships are radically ruptured, major structural change is impossible, and because social democrats are not willing or able to do this, that, in essence, is why social democratic parties in Government have nowhere near achieved their aims.

Miliband raises this problem of the apparent failure of social democracy at one point in his book *The State in Capitalist Society*.[10] His concern is to explain the failure of political will, the lack of boldness with which social democratic governments have approached their task. Apart from the

---

[7] *ibid.*, p. 121.

[8] Anderson, P., 'Problems of Socialist Strategy' in Anderson, P., and Blackburn, R., (eds.), *Towards Socialism*, Fontana, 1965.

[9] Anderson, *op. cit.*, p. 234.

[10] Miliband, R., *The State in Capitalist Society*, Wiedenfeld & Nicolson, 1969.

problem of leadership (which we return to below), he argues that this timidity is partly due to the fact that 'Labour', unless it freely uses the strike weapon, has not had anything like the power of 'Capital' when it comes to influencing the government of the day. Businessmen take crucial decisions about investment and production – giving them an immediate rapport with, for instance, civil servants – and any government, whatever its political complexion must therefore set out to obtain the 'confidence' of the business and financial community. In terms of public opinion, business can also *appear* to represent the general or 'National' interest, while Trade Unions appear only to represent a sectional interest.

These three contributions either argue or take as their basic assumption that social democratic parties, including the British Labour Party, have essentially failed to do what they ostensibly set out to do – to change substantially the reward structure of modern capitalism. Two main reasons are given for this failure: the nature of power and the state in capitalist society, and a lack of political will on the part of social democratic leaders. But the second is in turn partly explained by the first. For although some kind of will does exist, they say that it is the wrong one, based, among other things, on an incorrect analysis of power relationships. Even if the will really does exist in a much stronger form than the authors imagine, social democratic leaders would still be constrained and their policies emasculated by the normal operation of existing power relations within capitalist society. The arguments of Parkin, Anderson and Miliband therefore boil down to a general analysis of the social system as a whole. What they are essentially saying is that the social democratic parties in Western European countries have failed because they have been trying to reform capitalism piecemeal, rather than working towards the overthrow of it.

But if that is so, then one is entitled to ask, for instance, how the overthrow of capitalism *is* likely to come about. Indeed, it is possible to take issue with the authors on a number of aspects of their respective arguments – and from various points of view. For instance, from the point of view of historical interpretation, one could argue that to judge social democratic parties a 'failure' in that they have not done what they originally set out to do is difficult because there are a number of different interpretations of what precisely they *did* set out to do. Some people, for example, are under the impression that the Labour Party began as a radical socialist party, committed to the abolition of capitalism, which has since become 'de-radicalized' – but, as we shall see later, there is very little evidence supporting this assumption. From the sociological point of view, there is a need to clearly spell out just what these 'encircling pressures of capitalist society' are, and, assuming they exist, to show how they operate and to what effect. Finally, it is also possible to turn this kind of argument on its head and ask: if social democratic parties have not achieved very much in socialist terms, what would have? If the answer is a social revolution, what is the real likelihood of a revolution occurring in Britain today? Would the working class have responded to a revolutionary call in 1900? or in 1918? or 1945?

Despite these reservations, there is a sense in which the authors are correct, a sense in which the social democratic experience has been a disappointment for socialists. Some would even argue that we are now experiencing a 'decline' and 'de-radicalization' of social democratic politics, which would imply that the Labour Party is moving still further away from the socialist road – but the evidence for that assertion needs to be examined. It is, however, indisputable that seventy-five years of the Labour Party have not brought us very close to socialism – however it is defined. It would, therefore, seem worthwhile to explore ways of finding out why. Each of the authors cited, and many others as well, have made a contribution to answering this question – but there are still obvious gaps to be filled in our knowledge of the Labour Party. This is quite simply why I have chosen to focus on some aspects of the relationships between the Labour Party and the working class, beginning with a consideration of the electoral links between the two.

2. Working Class Voting Behaviour

The British Class Structure

In the Introduction the term 'working class' was frequently used. There are people who would argue today that terms like 'class', 'working class' and 'class war' are meaningless because classes no longer exist, and to talk about the 'working class' is to be out-of-date and really rather old-fashioned. I have heard Labour Cabinet Ministers and constituency activists say just this. A new vocabulary has come into fashion and modern euphemisms for working class are now 'working people', 'workpeople', 'ordinary families', 'the less well-off' and 'less privileged sections of the community'. These terms are frequently used by politicians and commentators for various reasons, but their unconscious effect is often to emasculate the original Marxist concept of class as a structural feature of capitalist society and to disguise or underestimate the extent and significance of inequalities based on class.[1]

Most social scientists would reject the argument that classes no longer exist, and since the debates about the 'affluent worker' and increasing 'middleclassness' in the late 1950s and early 1960s, most would now agree that the extent of class inequality is still great, although they would not necessarily agree on its social or political significance. But nobody who is interested in the study of society would deny that class is important, and there is a wealth of evidence to show that class and class-background largely determines a person's likely income attainment, type of housing accommodation, level of educational achievement, the kind of life they lead and

---

[1] For an account of how the ideological presuppositions of some academics (especially certain sociologists) have led them to underestimate the significance of class, and to ignore or dismiss continued inequalities of income, status and power, see Westergaard, J. H., 'The Withering Away of Class' in Anderson, P. and Blackburn, R. (eds.), *Towards Socialism*, Fontana, 1965, reprinted more recently (with a postscript) as 'Sociology: the Myth of Classlessness' in Blackburn, R., (ed.), *Ideology in Social Science*, Fontana, 1972.

the kind of things they are able to do. Practically every sphere of social life in Britain is in some way class-based, and so it is that class forms the very basis of party politics. As numerous authorities have noted, voting is pre-eminently related to class, and without the class dimension it is impossible to understand or explain the workings of the party political system.[2]

The best indicator and main component of class is occupation. Although knowledge of a person's occupation will not always tell us precisely what class that person is in, it is used by social scientists as a convenient short-hand for class because, in general, people who are in a similar occupation are also in the same class. Actually, there is a continuing and involved debate between those who accept the Marxist analysis that class is primarily determined by an individual's relationship to the means of production (whether the individual owns capital or merely sells his or her labour power), and those who follow the German sociologist Max Weber in arguing that class is more determined by one's status or standing in the community.[3] But all would agree that occupation is pre-eminently impor-

Distributions of Male Occupations U.K. 1913–14 to 1970[4]

(Occupations as % of total)

	1913/14	1922/24	1935/36	1955/56	1970
Employers	7·7	7·7	7·6	5·7	4·9
Professional:					
Higher	1·3	1·4	1·5	2·6	3·5
Lower	1·6	2·0	2·0	3·2	4·5
Managers	3·9	4·3	4·5	6·7	7·5
Clerks	5·5	5·4	5·5	6·3	7·0
Foremen	1·7	1·9	2·0	3·7	5·0
Skilled Manual	33·0	32·3	30·0	30·4	25·0
Semi-skilled	33·6	28·3	28·8	27·9	24·5
Unskilled	11·5	16·7	17·9	13·8	15·0
All males	100	100	100	100	100

(Self-employed not included)

[2] See Blondel, J., *Voters, Parties and Leaders: The Social Fabric of British Politics*, Pelican, 1963 new edn., 1975; Butler, D., and Stokes, D., *Political Change in Britain: Forces Shaping Electoral Choice*, Pelican, 1971; Pulzer, P. G. J., *Political Representation and Elections in Britain*, Allen and Unwin, 1967.

[3] A good point to start would be Bottomore, T. B., *Classes in Modern Society*, Allen and Unwin, 1965, followed by Dahrendorf, R., *Class and Class Conflict in Industrial Society*, Routledge, 1959, and Giddens, A., *The Class Structure of Advanced Societies*, Hutchinson, 1973.

[4] From Barratt Brown, M., *From Labourism to Socialism: The Political Economy of Labour in the 1970s*, Spokesman, 1972, Table 6. I, p. 147, in turn taken mainly from Routh, G., *Occupation and Pay in Great Britain 1906–1960*, (London, C.U.P., 1965).

tant, and that the occupational structure of a society like Britain is the backbone of the class structure, and hence of the wider society.

If we look at the occupational structure of Britain we find that there are a very large number of manual workers, skilled, semi-skilled or unskilled, and that they form by far the largest proportion of the workforce. As the table on page 9 shows, in 1970, manual workers constituted nearly seven-tenths of the male working population. This proportion has declined steadily since 1913/14, but it was not until the 1960s that non-manual white collar workers of all kinds actually formed more than 30 per cent of the total, and it has been estimated that this proportion is only likely to reach about 36 per cent by 1981.[5] Compared with other European and advanced industrial societies, Britain is unique in two respects. First, only a small proportion of the working population are engaged in agriculture, and therefore there is no significant rural peasant class. Second, and related to this, Britain has a relatively small number of employers and self-employed persons in the working population because there is no property-owning peasantry or significant petit bourgeois. In terms of *economic* class, therefore, Britain has a large and mainly urban working class which accounts for some 80 per cent of the employed population, a small owning and managing class (about 10 per cent) and a small professional and supervisory class (about 10 per cent).[6]

Other classifications based on occupation are possible, of course, and most social scientists and market researchers prefer to use four or five main categories – professional and managerial, intermediate non-manual (teachers, supervisors), skilled manual and routine white collar (clerks, shop assistants), semi-skilled manual, and unskilled manual workers. For opinion poll and market research purposes, the routine white collar workers are included in the intermediate non-manual category and the unskilled and pensioners are lumped together, giving the four familiar groups of AB (professional/managerial), C1 (white collar), C2 (skilled manual) and DE (unskilled manual). Social scientists more frequently use five categories and keep the routine white collar workers in the same group as the skilled manuals, because in terms of earnings and status these two groups are more alike. On the other hand, many would argue that the key division in the occupational structure is between manual and non-manual, primarily because of differences in hours worked, working conditions, holidays and other fringe benefits. But no matter which way occupations are classified,

---

[5] Barratt Brown, M., *op. cit.*, p. 18.

[6] *ibid.*, p. 19.

or what the categories are called, they all reveal the existence of a very large manual working class.[7]

Moreover, not only does Britain have a large manual working class, the size of which has remained pretty much the same over the last sixty years, the income differentials between the classes and occupational groups have also proved to be remarkably durable, despite the rise of Labour. Apart from the routine white collar workers already mentioned, those above the skilled manual category in the following table have nearly always taken home more than the average earnings (100) in each period, and those below have always taken home less.

Male Occupational Earnings U.K. 1913/14 to 1970[8]

(Earnings as % of average in each period)

	1913/14	1922/23	1935/36	1955/56	1970
Professional:					
Higher	365	375	344	243	252
Lower	172	178	166	96	105
Managers	218	268	236	234	230
Clerks	110	101	103	82	85
Foremen	126	150	145	124	126
Skilled manual	110	100	105	98	99
Semi-skilled	76	70	72	74	72
Unskilled	70	72	69	69	67
All males	100	100	100	100	100

While the continuing differences in personal earnings are one major source of the perpetuation of inequality, the unequal distribution of personal wealth is another. Despite the introduction of progressive income tax, death duties and similar measures, the distribution of wealth has not markedly changed during the course of the twentieth century as the following table suggests.

---

[7] See, for instance, an analysis of the 1951 Census in terms of class and socio-economic group in Cole, G. D. H., *Studies in Class Structure*, Routledge, 1955, p. 153; also the 1961 Census in Martin, D., and Crouch, C., 'England' in Archer, M. A., and Giner, S. (eds.), *Contemporary Europe: Class Status and Power*, Wiedenfeld and Nicolson, 1971, p. 247.

[8] Barratt Brown, *op. cit.*, p. 147.

Distribution of Personal Wealth in U.K. 1911–1967[9]

Percentage of population	1911–13	Percentages of total personal wealth		
		1936–38	1960	1963–67
1	69	56	42	29
5	87	79	75	54
10	92	88	83	67

All the factual evidence therefore suggests that Britain is as deeply divided as ever in terms of occupation, income, and wealth. Around 70 per cent of the working population have manual occupations. These 70 per cent not only tend to get paid less than non-manual workers, who only constitute around 30 per cent of the workforce, but their jobs are frequently more unpleasant, have less status attached to them, and there are usually fewer fringe benefits. This in many ways is a more visible division in British society than others based on concepts like 'economic class', and the terms 'middle class' and 'working class' are frequently used synonymously with 'non-manual' and 'manual', although, as we have seen, this is not strictly accurate.

Another way in which this key division is more obvious than others is that most people tend to perceive the class structure as being divided on a two-fold basis. Studies of how people see classes and how they see themselves fitting into the class structure ('subjective stratification') have demonstrated the prime importance of the 'middle class' and 'working class' categories based on the manual/non-manual distinction. For instance, Runciman showed that manual workers on the whole tend to describe themselves as working class, while non-manual workers are more likely to describe themselves as middle class, although each individual's opinion will be slightly modified by things like their actual level of income and type of housing accommodation:

Self-Assigned Class by Occupation[10]

	Non-manual %	Manual %
Upper or Upper middle	6	—
Middle	51	22
Lower Middle	10	7
Working	19	52
Don't know, Other, None, etc.	14	19

[9] Revell, J. R. S., 'Changes in the social distribution of property in Britain during the twentieth century', *Actes du Troisième Congrès International d'Histoire Economique*, Munich, 1965. 1963–67 estimate, which excludes state pensions, from Atkinson, A. B., *Unequal Shares* (Pelican, 1974) p. 14. The author states that these figures, if anything, underestimate the degree of concentration.

[10] Runciman, W. G., *Relative Deprivation and Social Justice*, Routledge, 1966, p. 158.

Butler and Stokes, in their major study of party political attitudes, also stressed the widespread acceptance of this two-fold model of the class structure, affirming 'the extraordinary hold of this dichotomy' which seems to be deeply rooted in the mind of the ordinary British citizen'.[11] Their figures, suggesting that some 67 per cent of the population would describe themselves as 'working class', 29 per cent 'middle class' or 'lower middle' class, and 4 per cent 'upper' or 'upper middle' class, also bears out the argument that the 'subjective' dimensions of stratification complement the objective facts. In addition, there are other respects, like the existence of different 'cultures' and 'communities', in which it could be said that Britain is divided into a large 'working class' and a smaller 'middle class'.

Class and Voting

What I wish to do here is to outline the links between the class structure and the party political system, focusing particularly on the relationship between social class and voting behaviour. We will then be in a position to look at two recent theories about how this is supposed to be changing, and its significance for the Labour Party. There may have been no 'decline' or disappearance of the working class as such, but what of the role of the working class in party politics?

In the book called *The Decline of Working Class Politics*, a study of Liverpool Labour Party written in the depths of disillusionment with the 1966–70 Labour government, one of the main conclusions of its author was that 'the close association between party and class has itself declined and, with the progressive disappearance of the class polarization of formal politics, there has been a decline in political activity resulting from identification with, and commitment to, the interests of the working class as such'.[12] This is one of the four key statements Hindess makes which sum up his overall argument that there has been a 'decline of working class politics'. The other three are outlined and placed in their context towards the end of this chapter. All four will be closely examined in turn, and we will return to them in the course of the book. The questions raised by his argument are not the only ones to be looked at, but they provide a useful starting point.

For the moment, I want to limit myself to the first part of the above statement which says that 'the close association between party and class has itself declined' and that there has been a 'progressive disappearance of

---

[11] Butler and Stokes, *op. cit.*, pp. 92–3.
[12] Hindess, *op. cit.*, p. 163.

the class polarization of formal politics' – and even then only from the point of view of voting behaviour.

Numerous studies and polls have affirmed that electoral behaviour in Britain, like other social behaviour, is predominantly class-based. As Pulzer has pointed out, class is the major dividing line in British society and the single most important determinant of social and political behaviour precisely because it is the *only* major dividing line in British society.[13] We lack the profound linguistic, racial and religious schisms which pre-occupy the minds of citizens of other nations. Perhaps the best way to see how class influences electoral behaviour is to look at the record since 1945, to see which way members of each class have tended to vote in General Elections. The following table is taken from Gallup Poll surveys at the time of each General Election (they were accurate to within 2 per cent between 1950 and 1966) and shows the range of voting for each social class:

Class Differences in Voting Behaviour 1945–1966[14]

Class and % of Total Vote (1966)	Conservative	Labour	Liberal
Upper Middle 3%	76–90%	6–14%	2–14%
Middle Class 22%	61–77%	16–24%	2–15%
Working Class 67%	32–44%	52–61%	2–14%
Very Poor 8%	23–44%	54–72%	2–12%

More sophisticated breakdowns of class and occupational categories, whether actual or self-described, will also reveal a near perfect gradation from Labour to Tory as we ascend the social ladder.[15]

Class may be the prime influence, but secondary factors are also important. First, voting is partially related to age.[16] Young people under 30 years of age, no matter what class they are born into, all tend to be more left-wing than their elders, i.e. more likely to vote Labour. It is interesting to note that they always have been to some extent, so this does not necessarily mean that they retain the habit as they get older, or that Labour will soon have a permanent parliamentary majority. As a matter of fact, middle-aged people have always tended to be more evenly balanced between Labour and Tory, while voters over the age of 50 have been more likely to vote

---

[13] Pulzer, *op. cit.*, p. 44.

[14] From Durant, H., 'Voting Behaviour in Britain 1945–66' in Rose, R. (ed.) *Studies in British Politics*, Macmillan, 1969 (2nd edn.). These figures differ slightly from the British Institute of Public Opinion data presented in Finer, S. E., *Comparative Government*, Allen Lane, 1970 and Pelican, 1974, p. 143.

[15] See Butler and Stokes, *op. cit.*, ch. 4., pp. 90–124.

[16] For the 1945–66 figures on age and sex see Durant, *op. cit.*, pp. 168–9.

Conservative. Second, voting is related to sex, and women of all ages are more likely than men to vote Conservative. Third, religion is important, especially in some areas of the country, and regular Anglican churchgoers, for instance, are also much more likely to vote Conservative. Fourth, other factors like regional and local traditions, house ownership, and the proportion of different classes in each community or neighbourhood, all help to explain voting patterns. Finally, and most important of all these secondary factors from the point of view of Labour voting, is the fact of Trade Union membership. Within the manual working class, Labour voting is more related to Trade Union membership than anything else. Unionized manual workers vote Labour in the proportion of about three or four to one, but non-unionized manual workers are about evenly split between Labour and Tory.

The realization that about half the non-unionized manual workers continue to vote Conservative led to the 'rediscovery' of the 'working class Tories' during the 1960s. This discovery was marked in academic circles by the publication of three important books – Runciman's *Relative Deprivation and Social Justice*, Nordlinger's *The Working Class Tories*, and McKenzie and Silver's *Angels in Marble*.[17] It was pointed out that even though the Labour Party was the working class party and commanded the electoral support of nearly two-thirds of the working class, the Conservatives were still getting half their total vote from working class voters. There could be no waning of socialist fervour or 'decline of working class politics' for them.

The problem, however, was to explain why as many as one-third or more of all working class electors apparently voted against their class interests, and a number of new factors came to light in these studies. Runciman, for instance, found that working class or middle class electors who describe themselves as 'middle class' are more likely to vote Conservative than those who describe themselves as 'working class'. While emphasizing this role of 'self-rated class' (Butler and Stokes call it 'class self-image'[18]), Runciman also found a clear link between Conservative voting and the kind of reason given for voting. When asked to explain why they vote the way they do, manual workers who concentrate on their job, class or status rather than, say, the intrinsic qualities of each party or the influence of family or friends,

---

[17] Runciman, *ot. cit.*; Nordlinger, E. A., *The Working Class Tories*, MacGibbon & Kee, 1967; McKenzie, R. T. and Silver, A., *Angels in Marble*, Heinemann, 1968.

[18] Butler and Stokes, *op. cit.*, p. 104, found that most working class Conservatives preferred to describe themselves as 'upper working class' rather than 'working class'.

turn out to be far more likely to vote Labour.[19] Tory voters on the other hand, especially Tory voters at the lower end of the social scale, appear to be far less interested in job, class or status considerations when they make up their mind to vote. More recently, Goldthorpe *et al.* have argued that for working class voters, their 'white-collar affiliations' are crucially important.[20] By this they mean the family, neighbourhood, and wider social relationships of each individual which involve contact with white-collar workers. Thus manual workers who have frequent contact with predominantly Tory-voting white-collar workers are more likely to vote Tory than those who rarely associate with people other than manual workers.

Nordlinger's approach had a different emphasis. He argued from survey data that while working class Conservatism was related to sex, religion, education, father's occupation, Trade Union membership and each individual's views on things like class conflict and royalty, the concept of 'middle class identification' was most useful in explaining why some working class people voted Conservative. He wrote:

> To state the conclusion in a sentence, a sense of economic well-being frequently leads to middle class identification because the workers define middle class people as economically secure and comfortable and see themselves as such; and in turn, middle class identification often results in Tory voting due to the dual belief that this is the 'proper' way for middle-class people to behave and that Tory measures are most likely to maintain their economic well-being.[21]

McKenzie and Silver claimed to have isolated two other distinctive attitudes among the working class Conservatives they interviewed. After exploring elector's views on a number of specific issues and their general approach to politics, they found that Tory and labour voters did not differ very much on most counts except that the attitudes of working class Conservatives tended to be of two kinds which they called 'deferential' and 'secular'. The deferential 'see the Conservative elite as the natural rulers of Britain — sensitive to her traditions and peculiarities, and uniquely qualified to govern by birth, experience and outlook',[22] whereas in the mind

---

[19] Runciman, *op. cit.*, pp. 180–1.

[20] Goldthorpe, J., Lockwood, D., Bechhofer, F., Platt, J., *The Affluent Worker (2): Political Attitudes and Behaviour*, Cambridge University Press, 1968.

[21] Nordlinger, *op. cit.*, p. 175.

[22] McKenzie and Silver, *op. cit.*, p. 242. Another aspect of deference was described by Wertheimer as the 'tenderly wistful interest in the vacuous doings of the upper ten thousand' — see Wertheimer, E., *Portrait of the Labour Party*, Putnam, 1929.

of the secular working class voter, the Conservative Party's elite are 'judged the best rulers on more pragmatic grounds' because they always demonstrate a 'superior performance in the arts of government'[23] and it is assumed that they will continue to deliver the goods more efficiently in the future. Whether the experience of 1970–4 has accelerated the erosion of deferential attitudes remains to be seen. But before then, the Butler and Stokes surveys of the early sixties produced convincing evidence to suggest that working class Conservatism was on the decline.[24] However, more recent surveys and polls have suggested that even this trend has now been checked and may be in reverse.

Of equal importance to the understanding of working class Conservatism is an explanation of working class Labour voting, and one famous study of Labour voting is worth noting. *Must Labour Lose?*[25] was produced in 1960 in response to the 'affluence' scare which afflicted the Labour Party and some social scientists soon after the 1959 General Election. Labour had just suffered its third successive election defeat, and the argument common at the time was that the workers weren't voting Labour in such great numbers as in the past because the Conservative administrations of the 1950s had made them all very affluent and contented. *Must Labour Lose?* is a good example of the Revisionist attempt to explain why Labour had apparently lost support in the previous ten years, although it ignored the fact that Labour had probably not lost much 'support' at all, but had marginally failed to mobilize its natural electorate. In any case, a drop in Labour's share of the poll from 46·1 per cent in 1950 to 43·8 per cent in 1959 was hardly catastrophic, and could scarcely herald the imminent demise of the Labour Party. Undaunted, the authors seemed determined to come up with an explanation suggesting that major changes in voting behaviour were already under way.

They began by pointing out, quite correctly, that the relationship between party and class is not a perfect one, and then proceeded to explore by means of a questionnaire survey the nature of the electoral allegiance of nearly two-thirds of the working class to Labour. Among other things, their survey results showed that while 89 per cent of Labour voters chose to describe the Labour Party as 'the party of the working class', only 27 per cent thought that this was one of the four most important features of the party. In fact, out of a comprehensive list of 'features' of the Labour Party, specifically 'class' concerns were only placed sixth, tenth and twelfth in

---

[23] McKenzie and Silver, *op. cit.*, p. 243.
[24] See Butler and Stokes, *op. cit.*, pp. 136–49.
[25] Abrams, M., Rose, R., and Hinden, R., *Must Labour Lose?*, Penguin, 1960.

order of importance, and the authors therefore concluded that 'present support for Labour largely stems from an unconsidered identification with the working class on the part of people who in fact are ready to attach much more importance to other facets of political life'.[26] The class attachment to Labour, they argue, is a 'fragile bond', a bond easily broken.

While this may or may not be true, the subsequent commentary by Rita Hinden took this useful survey data and super-imposed upon it a unique analysis of the changing class structure of Britain which managed to combine just about all the 'affluence' myths of the period. Basically, she argued that the working class was virtually disappearing, if it had not done so already.[27] Class was therefore no longer objectively important, and this was reflected in the alleged waning of Labour's class appeal. In consequence, she argued that Labour's image and politics needed to be drastically 'modernized', nationalization should be dropped, and socialism was redefined accordingly.[28]

In 1963–4, Goldthorpe and colleagues tested the assumptions of this argument using a sample of relatively affluent workers in Luton (mostly highly-paid car workers). Their conclusions were on the whole contrary to those of the 'Must Labour Lose?' school. Of the manual workers interviewed, no less than 79 per cent supported Labour, and there had been no rapid increase in the proportion of Conservative-voting white-collar workers.[29] The survey indicated a pretty stable working class loyalty to the Labour Party, with very little evidence of it having been eroded, as can be seen from the following figures on voting behaviour and intention:

	Manual Workers % of votes cast		White-collar Workers % of votes cast	
	Labour	Conservative	Labour	Conservative
1955	83	15	32	55
1959	80	16	30	55
Intention 1963–4	79	14	32	58

In giving reasons for this loyalty, a majority of the manual workers actually mentioned 'the working class' but they did so in such a way as to

---

[26] *ibid.*, p. 14; Compare Benney *et al.*'s 1949 study in Greenwich where 93 per cent of Labour voters agreed that it was the Labour Party which would do best for the working class, but only 42 per cent made direct reference to class interests when asked why they would vote Labour. See Benney, M., Gray, A. P., and Pear, R. H., *How People Vote – A Study of Electoral Behaviour in Greenwich*, Routledge, 1956, pp. 200–1.

[27] Abrams *et al.*, *op. cit.*, pp. 94–108, esp. pp. 100 and 105.

[28] *ibid.*, p. 121.

[29] Goldthorpe *et al.*, *op. cit.*, p. 13.

indicate that they did not think that there was really very much difference
between the parties.[30] Among other things, they also found that class consciousness in relation to the Trade Union and Labour movements was not
high, and political discussion between workmates and friends was relatively uncommon. But as regards the affluence theory, they found that no less
than 81 per cent of the *most* affluent and relatively satisfied workers still intended to vote Labour.[31] As noted above, they concluded that 'the understanding of contemporary working class politics is to be found, first and
foremost, in the structure of the worker's group attachments ("white-collar
affiliations") and not, as many have suggested, in the extent of his income
or possessions'.[32] Thus it appeared that Labour's electoral appeal to the
working class had not been eroded by economic changes. While some
Labour leaders were busily underplaying or ignoring the politics of class,
the class-based nature of Labour's electoral support remained essentially
the same.

Throughout this outline of the bare electoral facts, I have been careful
first, to describe what we have been talking about as the *party* political
system, in order to distinguish it from the wider political system of forces
and power relationships which help shape society and social institutions
like the political parties. Second, I have always referred to the *electoral*
support and *electoral* loyalty of certain sections of society toward the
political parties in order to distinguish this from other, deeper forms of
allegiance. This is partly because survey and poll evidence has consistently
revealed that a majority of the voting population do not hold their four or
five-yearly General Election vote in high regard. To most people, voting is
not a particularly meaningful act, a high proportion of voters see very little
difference between the parties, and most claim that they are not offered
enough choice. This is especially true of working class Labour voters, who
invariably turn out to be the most cynical section of the electorate. To speak,
therefore, of their 'loyalty' to the Labour Party, a party, which according to
survey evidence, most of them really don't think much of, is to use a mis-
nomer. It is this distinction between the *degree* of working class electoral
support, and the *quality* of working class allegiance to the Labour Party
which is so important, and failure to distinguish the two has frequently
resulted in confusion.

Thus, the *Must Labour Lose?* authors seemed to argue that a change in
the quality of working class allegiance to Labour was bringing about a

---

[30] *ibid.*, p. 46.
[31] *ibid.*, p. 18.
[32] *ibid.*, p. 82.

change in the degree of working class electoral support for Labour. In concentrating on the allegedly diluted quality of allegiance, they failed to recognize that the facts concerning the degree of working class electoral support did not really justify their case. As we shall see, Hindess made the same mistake. But, because his argument was more complex, and he was talking about the relationship between party and class at the electoral, parliamentary and constituency party levels simultaneously, he made this same mistake a number of times and in both directions, arguing from degree to quality and from quality to degree. On the other hand, Goldthorpe *et al.* successfully managed to differentiate both aspects, and demonstrated that, even among affluent workers, the degree of electoral support for Labour has apparently remained as high as ever. But they, like others, also had plenty to say about changes in the quality and flavour of working class politics, and it is to a preliminary consideration of this we will now turn.

The Decline of Working Class Politics?

A number of writers over recent years have argued that the traditional relationship between Labour and the working class is breaking down in more significant ways, especially in terms of the diluted ideological flavour and meaning of Labour politics. While the Labour Party has lost its sense of purpose, the working class as a whole have lost their radicalism. Both have become 'de-radicalized' in the sense that they no longer present a threat to the existing order of capitalist society, and traditional socialist doctrine is no longer espoused quite so frequently or with quite so much enthusiasm.

One version of this argument is contained in the 'affluent worker' thesis, which, as we have seen, essentially says that the working class have lost their radicalism because absolute standards of living have risen, although successively less-than-radical Labour leaderships have accelerated the process. The second version is contained in the 'decline of working class politics' thesis, which argues that the working class have 'seen through' the 'fraud' of Social Democracy as a result of the somewhat inglorious history of the Labour Party and, at all levels, they are increasingly refusing to play any part in it. Once again, successive Party leaderships are partly to blame, but changes at the local level are seen as integral to the 'de-radicalization' process.

More often than not, those who have referred to the alleged process have done so in such a way as to give the impression that they are stating the obvious, that this 'de-radicalization' is a self-evident truth which requires no supporting evidence. For instance, Parkin attempts to account for the phenomenon without really showing that it has in fact occurred, although he does demonstrate that mass working class parties like the British Labour Party have not been very successful in making an impact on the reward structure' of western societies.[33] Epstein states categorically that much of the shift in party posture in Britain and in other nations has been in the form of a continued dilution, now almost liquidation, of traditional Socialist doctrine', without providing any evidence.[34] But – as we shall see in the next chapter – none of these arguments are particularly new, and people have variously argued that the Labour Party has lost its socialism, was about to be deserted by the workers, and was on the point of disappearing into oblivion ever since it began. However, the two theories cited here have been particularly common over recent years, and have proved too influential to be ignored.

The 'affluent worker' debate of the 1960s was really part of the larger, continuing debate between sociologists and marxists, and between social democrats and Revolutionaries on the revolutionary potential of the working class.[35] The 'affluent worker' theorists sought to show that the economic, technological, managerial and demographic changes since 1945 had led to the 'embourgeoisement' of the working class. Economic changes had brought about rising living standards, the growth of a new middle class, and the decline of the traditional working class. Technological changes had purportedly increased the number of white collar jobs and had broken down the manual/non-manual distinction. New managerial techniques had supposedly created better industrial relations, and changes in the urban environment in the form of suburban development and the demolition of central urban areas had led to the break-up of traditional working-class communities. The growing influence of the mass media, especially commercial television, had encouraged the feeling that 'we are all middle class now'. Against this background, socialism, as an alternative way of organizing the social system, seemed to be really quite out of the question and the Labour Party trimmed its policies to meet the new situation.

---

[33] Parkin, op. cit., p. 103: '. . . the history of the European Socialist parties is a chronicle of the gradual and continuous dilution of (these) early radical aims'.

[34] Epstein, L. D., Political Parties in Western Democracies, Pall Mall, 1967, p. 156.

[35] For an introduction to this debate see Mann, M., Consciousness and Action Among the Western Working Class, Macmillan, 1973.

The problem, however, was that none of these changes were occurring t‹ anything like the extent that had been suggested, and when detailed studie‹ were undertaken, focusing on specific examples of these alleged changes, i‹ was found that they were by no means as significant as had been thought‹ For instance, highly paid manual workers were not really becomin‹ 'middle-class' in any real sense at all, and the basic position of the manua‹ worker in the class structure and in the local community remained muc‹ the same. And we have already shown that the combination of these allege‹ changes had not led to the predicted decline in Labour voting. In fact, a‹ early as 1961, a point by point refutation of the argument that affluenc‹ automatically led to Tory voting had been provided by Mark Abrams, th‹ man who had carried out the research for the unfortunate *Must Labou‹ Lose?* [36] But the major failing of these theories was that they presente‹ economic and political trends in a simple relation of cause and effect. The‹ implied that socialist commitment always declined when economic con‹ ditions improved, and vice-versa.

This was challenged by a number of writers including Ralph Miliband‹ who wrote in 1964 that

> 'the evidence is altogether lacking that the "affluence" of the last decad‹
> has produced a marked decline in working-class militancy or in socialis‹
> commitment, as compared with the unaffluent past. In any case, poverty
> and "affluence", taken by themselves are far too abstract categories t‹
> serve as explanations of social behaviour and commitment. Just as th‹
> belief that poverty as such produces militant reactions is contradicte‹
> by the evidence, so the attribution to "affluence" of a soporific socia‹
> effect is equally doubtful'. [37]

Indeed, Miliband goes on to say that greater affluence, far from being ‹ bar to socialist development, may in fact be a precondition, 'for experience strongly suggests that it is only *after* elementary needs have ceased to be ar‹ incessant, gnawing preoccupation, that the socialist critique of capitalism may carry conviction.' [38] Moreover, in relation to the alleged changes in the urban environment, Westergaard pointed out that the existence o‹ geographically and socially isolated working class communities in the past may also have acted as a bar to socialist development because they created‹

---

[36] Abrams, M., 'Social Class and British Politics', in *Public Opinion Quarterly*, 1961, vol. XX, no. ‹ pp. 342–50.

[37] Miliband, R., 'Socialism and the Myth of the Golden Past', in *Socialist Register 1964*, Merli‹ Press, 1964, pp. 100–1.

[38] *ibid.*, p. 102. Cf. Lichtheim, G., *A Short History of Socialism*, Weidenfeld, 1970, p. 329.

parochial horizons and fostered a consciousness of community rather than class.[39] Urban redevelopment and the spread of the mass media would tend to widen those horizons.

Finally, another kind of critique of the affluence thesis argued that to speak of the 'new' working class and the 'old' or 'traditional' working class is nonsense because there is still a clearly identifiable working class, identifiable in terms of occupation, income, wealth and culture, and most important of all, one which still has the same relationship to the system of production. As Davis and Cousins pointed out at a recent conference, 'To be a proletarian is not to be pauperized but to be a commodity'.[40]

In various ways, therefore, the 'Affluent Worker' thesis did not appear to hold water. It had over-rated the significance of the economic and social changes that were occurring, and had drawn unjustified conclusions. Authors associated with it had assumed that socialist ideology was no longer the great motivating force it had been. More often than not, these conclusions were drawn in an attempt to justify a particular political position, and were not always based on 'disinterested' or 'objective' scientific research. In particular, the 'Affluent Worker' thesis was associated with elements on the right-wing of the Labour Party, the 'Revisionists', who used it to justify their argument that the Labour Party should be 'brought up-to-date' and given a new, more 'moderate' image. The revisionist debate within the Labour Party continued throughout the late 50s and early 60s, reaching a peak in 1960–1 when an attempt was made to revise the Party Constitution by dropping Clause IV. In many different forms, it is still with us today.

So is the second main version of the 'de-radicalization' argument, the 'decline of working class politics' thesis. But before I outline it in more detail, it should be placed firmly in its historical context. Just as the 'Affluent Worker' argument was a product of the 'affluent' fifties, so the experience of the 1966–70 Labour government is crucial to our understanding of the origins and appeal of the 'decline of working class politics'.

Between 1966 and 1970, the Labour Party broke faith with whole sections of its 'natural' constituency, including the trade unions, working-class militants, middle-class radicals, and youth. This profound disillusionment with Labour's performance in power has been used to account for such phenomena as the student revolt, the growth of Left groups, renewed

---

[39] Westergaard, *op. cit.*, p. 148.
[40] Davis, R. L., and Cousins, J. M., 'The "New Working Class" and the Old', in *Proceedings of the Social Science Research Council Conference: The Occupational Community of the Traditional Worker*, Durham, 1973.

interest in 'community action' and social work, the decline of constituency
party membership and activism, and widespread public apathy and
cynicism. The prevailing political cynicism at the time was reflected in an
NOP survey conducted in February 1968 prior to Labour's crushing
defeats in the local elections of May 1968. Despite the inherent problems of
validity in these kind of surveys, the extreme figures are particularly
illuminating.

Attitude	*% Agreeing*
Most politicians promise anything to get votes	78
Most politicians care more about their party than their country	66
Politicians are all talk and no action	59
Most politicians are in it for what they can get	57
Once MPs are elected, they forget about the voters	55

In that same year, the platform was defeated six times at the Annual
Conference of the Labour Party compared with once in 1967, twice in
1966, and not at all in 1964 and 1965.

But disenchantment among Labour supporters had set in long before
1968. As early as spring 1965, an issue of the socialist magazine *Views* was
devoted entirely to 'Britain in Labour', and asked: 'Are we to live by values
in the new Britain?'.[41] It continued:

> The essential improvisation of the 'scientific revolution' has narrow
> limits both of intention and theory. One sees, from Transport House
> reorganization and Ministerial statements, no sign of long-term plans of
> a more than electoral nature. And at the level of ideas, the Party seems
> unable to conceive either a Socialist pattern for particular social sectors,
> or for the whole social revolution it should be undertaking.[42]

By spring 1966, the magazine's editors were still repeating: 'We are not
saying merely that Wilson's Government is doing too little, too slowly. We
argue that it is not on the Socialist road at all'.[43]

By late 1966, this feeling had spread from the peripheral groupings to
more established pressure-groups within the Party. In the autumn of 1966,
three eminent Labour social scientists gave lectures to the Fabian Society
condemning respectively Labour's social plans, the operation of the
Welfare State, and the continued existence of poverty under Labour.[44]

---

[41] Editorial, *Views*, Spring 1965, no. 7, p. 2.
[42] *ibid.*, p. 4.
[43] Editorial, *Views*, Spring 1966, no. 10, p. 6.
[44] Abel-Smith, B., Townsend, P., Titmuss, R., and Crossman, R. H. S., *Socialism and Affluence Four Fabian Essays*, Fabian Society, London, 1967.

Professor Townsend summed up the feeling: 'The Labour Government is compromising too readily with entrenched interests, is avoiding the need to confront racial and social prejudice with moral authority, is failing to introduce institutional change . . .'[45] The main reason for this, Labour leaders argued at the time, was that the government was faced with an unprecedented economic crisis. But the consequence, as Lapping among others pointed out, was 'the worst sufferers from the economic difficulties were low-paid workers and pensioners, groups that the Government were particularly concerned to help'.[46] And Barratt Brown summed up the period 1964–70 as a failure to 'manage the economy in a way that benefited ordinary people.'[47] Whatever were the reasons for this key failure, it provided the objective basis for the rapid erosion of Labour's support.

Apart from the electoral disasters, nowhere was this collapse of support more obvious than in the Party's own constituency section. As McKie wrote, 'too much had been sacrificed for many to stomach. The monument to it all could be seen in the empty committee room, the lapsed membership, the tireless activist of former years now nodding gently before the television screen; also in the success of the Nationalist and Far Left groups . . .'[48] Ken Coates is a good example of the Labour Party activists who wrote profusely on the 'betrayal' of the Labour government in these years. His collection of essays is an interesting account of one individual's struggle against the policies of the leadership and the alienation of the rank and file. Already in 1967 he had noted 'the process of bleeding which has set in throughout the constituency section of the Party. How many thousands of good Socialists have withdrawn in disgust? . . . certainly there have been heavy losses . . .'[49]

Perhaps the most challenging analysis of the process of collapse in this period was provided in the May Day Manifesto, produced by a group of Labour academics and intellectuals, originally founded in 1966. This was a 'counter-statement to the Labour Government's policies and explanations' for those concerned with 'the effective introduction into political argument

---

[45] *ibid.*, p. 68. Another group of Labour academics writing in the depths of 1968 gave Labour a 'last chance' on 'matters of principle': 'What we all agree on is . . . that our Government has lacked idealism and principle, and that is central failure'. Burgess, T., *et al.*, *Matters of Principle – Labour's Last Chance*, Penguin, 1968, p. 8.

[46] Lapping, B., *The Labour Government 1964–70*, Penguin, 1970, p. 16.

[47] Barratt Brown, M., *From Labourism to Socialism*, Spokesman, 1972, p. 12.

[48] McKie, D., and Cook, C. (eds.), *The Decade of Disillusion: Politics in the Sixties*, Macmillan, 1972, p. 4.

[49] Coates, K., *The Crisis of British Socialism*, Spokesman, 1971, pp. 181–2.

and activity in Britain of a contemporary socialist case'.[50] It argued that the Labour Party had been assimilated into the structures of modern capitalism, and had degenerated into an 'alien form', a 'voting machine' and an 'effective bureaucracy' claiming no more than to run the existing system more efficiently. While it may seem strange to find obviously learned people putting forward this argument as if it were something entirely new, and as if this 'assimilation' and 'degeneration' had occurred quite recently, they did argue convincingly that for many socialists the Labour government experience had created a new situation, and had confirmed their worst fears:

> It has been clear for a long time that the Labour Party is a compromise between working class objectives and the traditional power structure: the first, it has often been hoped, could be achieved through the second. It has been possible in the past to see this as a necessary tension: the only way change can come. But what is more and more evident is that, in effective politics, this tension has gone.[51]

Another kind of tension, that between the major political parties themselves, had also gone, according to many political analysts and commentators. Indeed, the 'no difference' argument became exceptionally prevalent at the time. As Butler and Pinto-Duschinsky put it: 'The leaders of both parties, either from principle or with their eyes on the electorate, had in practice, if not explicitly, steered towards the middle. The real clashes of principle in 1966–70 and in the (1970 General Election) campaign seemed extraordinarily few'.[52] This became, in turn, one of the main reasons put forward to explain Labour's defeat in 1970. For instance, Crouch argued that while Labour was right to try and replace the Conservative Party as the natural governing party of Britain,

> 'there is little purpose, however, in a social democratic party seeking to become the party of the national consensus simply by adopting the policies of its opponents. Not only does this involve a complete loss of purpose in the party itself, it is also likely to fail. An electorate may well decide that a Conservative Party is a better party to head a conservative consensus.'[53]

---

[50] Williams, Raymond (ed.), *The May Day Manifesto 1968*, Penguin 1968, pp. 9–10. This was an enlarged version of the original 1967 statement.

[51] *ibid.*, p. 156.

[52] Butler, D., and Pinto-Duschinsky, M., *The British General Election of 1970*, Macmillan, 1971, p. xiv.

[53] Crouch, C., *Politics in a Technological Society*, Young Fabian Pamphlet, no. 23, Fabian Society, London, 1970, p. 18.

During this period, Barry Hindess was completing his book *The Decline of Working Class Politics*, which was based primarily on a study of Liverpool City Labour Party. His argument was that 'the Labour Party now appears to be less of a (working) class party than at any time in its history', and this is reflected in the increasingly middle-class leadership and rank and file. Party differences are based less and less on class loyalty, and 'it is more difficult than ever to see the Labour Party as the political arm of the working class movement, just as the Tories are no longer the political arm of militant *laissez-faire* Capitalism.' His 'major theme' is that two types of change, in the personnel of politics and in the nature of the Labour–Conservative dichotomy are intimately related, and are but aspects of 'wider developments in the overall character of contemporary politics' like the ever-increasing centralization of decision-making.[54] But the essential point was that the class character of party politics is declining, and the traditional allegiance of the working class to the Labour Party is breaking down.

In Liverpool, Hindess analysed the operation of the City Labour Party, first, by dividing the wards into predominantly 'working class' and 'middle class' areas, and showing that activity had declined in the former and risen in the latter since the early 1950s. Second, he attempted to demonstrate that the Labour Party members in these two types of ward had different local interests, different political concerns, and different overall policy orientations. For instance, members in the 'middle class' wards were less interested in the housing problem, and because the 'middle class' wards were strongest, and their members were strongly placed in the City Party machinery, 'working class' issues like housing tended to be ignored by the City Party and Council Group in favour of 'middle class' issues like education and traffic management. This had led, said Hindess, to a vicious circle of decline in working class participation in the ward parties in Liverpool and the growth of Far Left groups, and was symptomatic of a general decline in working class interest in party politics, an alienation from bourgeois democracy. He suggests that parliamentary democracy is becoming increasingly irrelevant to large numbers of working-class people, and the present 'party game' and 'election confidence trick' will, 'in common with other mass spectator sports . . . resort increasingly to gimmicks in order to draw the crowds'.[55]

The Hindess study, therefore, is 'an attempt to identify and clarify some

---

[54] Hindess, *op. cit.*, p. 179.
[55] *ibid.*, p. 179.

of the processes involved in the changing nature of British politics since the last war.'[56] Out of a welter of jumbled and complex argument, it is possible to isolate four substantive statements which deserve to be looked at in more detail because the arguments so contained have gained a certain amount of currency in academic and Labour Party circles within the last few years.

The first involves electoral turnout, party membership, and political participation:

'There has been in many areas, an absolute decline in voting and in other forms of orthodox political activity'.

The second, third and fourth all involve the relationship between party and class. The second is really the 'decline of working-class politics' thesis:

'The close association between party and social class has itself declined and, with the progressive disappearance of the class polarization of formal politics, there has been a decline in political activity resulting from identification with, and commitment to, the interests of the working class as such'.

The third involves changes in the Labour Party at the local level, which includes the 'middle-class takeover' argument:

'Changes in the Labour Party and in the urban environment have led to the differentiation of the political demands, concerns and orientations of party members and supporters in the different areas'.

The fourth involves the traditional allegiance of working-class people to the Labour Party:

'... the fact that the issues themselves are increasingly raised outside the formal political organisations ... marks the breakdown of that social control which the Labour Party has been able to exercise over such a large section of the population'.[57]

These assertions will be examined in relation to other evidence at various stages in this book, and so for the moment I will confine myself to two points. First, as we have seen, Hindess was writing in 1968–9, a period of spectacular decline in Labour Party support, a period in which activists were leaving in droves, individual CLP organizations were collapsing, and

---

[56] *ibid.*, p. 167.
[57] *ibid.*, pp. 163, 164, 172.

nationally the Labour Party was losing members at the rate of over 30,000 per year. It is not surprising, therefore, that Hindess was tempted to prophecy doom for the Labour Party, and predict a 'long-term decline of active Labour support among many sections of the working-class',[58] as so many had done before. Second, Hindess was concerned with the workings of the Labour Party in Liverpool, which, as Baxter forcefully argued in an article in *Political Studies* in March 1972,[59] has a unique history among big city Labour Parties, a history of factionalism rooted in religious sectarianism, of Irish immigrant aspirations, 'boss politics', weak organization, and extraordinarily low levels of participation. The last two features were highlighted by the Transport House Inquiries of 1939, 1953 and 1961, and the Liberal victories in the municipal elections of 1973. In addition, a survey by McKenzie in 1953 showed that the Liverpool-Scotland Constituency had the lowest ratio of Labour members to electors out of eighty-one Lancashire and Cheshire constituencies.[60] Furthermore, study after study has shown that Labour members are more active in their ward associations than their Conservative counterparts. There is one exception. Berry found the opposite in *The Sociology of Grass Roots Politics*,[61] and that was a study of Liverpool, Walton.

The Hindess study must, therefore, be treated with caution because of the uniqueness of Liverpool, and the specific characteristics of the period in which the study was undertaken. But, like so many similar arguments, the hidden assumption behind *The Decline of Working Class Politics* is that somehow things were much 'better' in the past, that there was much more activity of all kinds at the local level, that Labour ideology today is a palid, diluted version of what went before. As Miliband argued, the assumption is that there was a 'golden past', a golden age of socialist politics, and the subsequent story of the Labour Party and socialist thought in Britain has been one of a steady 'decline' and 'de-radicalization'. However, there is much evidence to suggest that this is a misreading of history, and that it stems from a misunderstanding of what the Labour Party is, and what it always has been. It is to a consideration of some problems arising out of the origins and history of the Labour Party that we now turn.

---

[58] *ibid.*, p. 120.

[59] Baxter, R., 'The Working Class and Labour Politics', *Political Studies*, 1972, vol. xx, no. 1, pp. 97–107.

[60] McKenzie, R. T., *British Political Parties*, Heinemann, 2nd edn., p. 545.

[61] Berry, D., *The Sociology of Grass Roots Politics*, Macmillan, 1970.

3. Understanding the Labour Party

'Those of us who wish to be relevant and topical sometimes need reminding that the most usual explanation of why a thing is as it is, is that things happened in the past to make it so.'[1]

The Labour Party. The very name is guaranteed to conjure up different images in the mind. The party for Labour, the party of Labour, the struggle to get labouring men and their representatives into Parliament. This was a simple image, but a dominant theme which inspired and pre-occupied the founders and early supporters of the Labour Party. Then came the adoption of 'socialism' in 1918, and the Labour Party became a socialist party, a party for socialism. Yet the Labour Party is, and always has been, infinitely more complex than any of these simple images would have us believe. It is this complexity which also defies any simple descrip-tion or explanation of the Labour Party, either in terms of its origins, sub-sequent evolution, or contemporary character.

Nevertheless, in this chapter I will attempt a short, general statement on the Labour Party, and one which places the contemporary Labour Party and the controversies which surround it into some kind of perspective. This will involve, in the first instance, an outline of the historical background to the perennial problems and dilemmas of the Labour Party, and second, an examination of the evidence and arguments relevant to the theories mentioned above. One methodological problem is that too many writers on the Labour Party have been concerned with prescriptive statements about what it ought to be rather than what it actually is, although of course, it is not always possible to divorce the two. A historical perspective is crucial here, because, as Ralph Miliband has argued: 'The assumption is often made in discussions of the Labour Party that the

---

[1] Crick, B., in the General Editor's Preface to Bealey, F. (ed.), *The Social and Political Thought of the Labour Party*, Weidenfeld and Nicolson, 1970, p. xi.

latter's difficulties are of recent origin. This is not so. In fact, what is so remarkable about the Labour Party is the similarity of the problems which have beset it throughout its history.'[2]

The Origins and Character of Labourism

The Founding Conference of the Labour Representation Committee was held on Thursday, 27 February 1900, in the Memorial Hall, Farringdon Street, London. The accredited delegates numbered 129, representing sixty-five trade unions and three socialist societies. The sixty-five trade unions claimed a total of 568,000 members, only about one third of the total membership of trade unions affiliated to the TUC and a mere fraction of all the workers in the country. Of the socialist societies represented, the Independent Labour Party claimed 13,000 members, the Social Democratic Federation 9,000 and the Fabians – who later proved to be so influential – had a national membership of precisely 861.

The Conference had been called as a result of a motion passed by the narrow margin of 546,000 to 434,000 at the TUC Conference in the previous September. It had been proposed and seconded at the TUC by a railway worker and a docker, but the motion had actually been drafted by Keir Hardie and Ramsay MacDonald in the offices of the Independent Labour Party. The goal of the ILP leaders was to forge an alliance between the socialist societies and the growing trade unions without alienating the highly pragmatic and mostly Liberal supporting Trade Union leaders. The motion therefore merely stated that the Special Conference was being called with the modest aim of 'securing a better representation of the interests of labour in the House of Commons'. Even this was nearly defeated by the cautious Trade Unionists, and in order to prevent the motion from being forgotten altogether, Hardie and MacDonald had to ensure that the Joint Committee of the TUC Parliamentary Committee and the Socialist Societies, which was to consider the motion, had a manipulated majority of sympathetic members. The aim of the Joint Committee was to get the Special Conference to accept the idea of a separate, autonomous Labour Group in parliament and this was duly achieved at the Memorial Hall, but only after a fundamental dispute over the nature of that group had been resolved. Some delegates wanted to restrict Labour candidacies to working men only, others to only those who recognized the existence of the class

---

[2] Miliband, R., *Parliamentary Socialism*, Merlin, 1972, p. 16.

war, but Hardie persuaded the Conference to accept a middle way which simply involved the acceptance of all candidates who said that they were sympathetic to the aims of the whole Labour movement, and would also be willing to join a distinct Labour Group in parliament which would engage 'in promoting legislation in the direct interest of Labour'. Hardie's amendment therefore avoided antagonizing the Trade Unionists afraid of pure socialism, and also left the way open for further developments in a socialist direction. This was a crucial decision in many ways and, as Francis Williams pointed out, 'the principles it embodied determined the composition of the Labour Party for many years'.[3]

In particular, it left the content and scope of the Labour Party's programme to the Parliamentary Group to decide upon, which Williams attributes to the delegates' 'practical wisdom and their understanding of the British political character'. He continues:

> that character thrives best in a constitutional framework which does not impose upon it the rigidness of a doctrinaire philosophy or even of a narrowly defined programme, but leaves, instead, sufficient freedom for the interpretation of events and needs and the common-sense application of fundamental philosophies according to the circumstances of the time.[4]

In this early decision of the LRC, we can therefore see the origins of the freedom of the PLP, the apparent lack of concern with ideologies and specific programmes, an implicit faith in the correctness of the 'aims' of the 'Labour movement', and the placing of the emergent Labour Party firmly within the traditions of the British Constitution and political culture.

The reasons for this are many, and they are to do with why Hardie and his comrades wanted to create a 'Labour Party' in the first place. For it is important to realize that the move to form an alliance between socialist societies and the trade unions only came about after other socialist movements had failed. In fact, the founding of the Labour Representation Committee came at a time of intense political reaction. The socialist groups most involved in the flowering of socialist activity and propaganda in the 1880s and 1890s had spent themselves, and had seemingly failed to make any headway, especially among the working class. Membership of the ILP and SDF had already begun to level-off and this trend continued into the first decade of the new century. As Williams wrote:

---

[3] Williams, F., *Fifty Years March – the Rise of the Labour Party*, Odhams, 1950, p. 23.
[4] *ibid.*, p. 25.

It is one of the ironies of the period that although the impact of the Fabian philosophy and the ILP crusading spirit upon the political and social life of the community and upon the outlook of the Labour movement had been immense, the actual membership of the socialist societies remained amazingly and disappointingly small.[5]

Hardie and his comrades realized this only too well. They argued that the key problem of taking the new socialist doctrine to the working class had not been overcome by the socialist societies, and a new way had to be found. First, they would have to create an alliance with the Trade Unions. Such an alliance would almost certainly involve ideological compromise, but it would gain through their established strength and continuity. Second, the new way would also be made possible by the likelihood of an ever-expanding franchise which would soon give the vote to more and more working people. Ramsay MacDonald, for instance, explicitly argued that 'the voting strength of this movement will come from the ranks of labour – the organized intelligent workers'.[6] Third, the inflexibility of the Liberals and the continued domination of political participation by the middle classes convinced Hardie and his ILP comrades that a new political party was becoming both necessary and possible. But in this respect, the historian Henry Pelling has argued that their motivation was based not so much on an abstract philosophical case for socialism but a realization of 'the failure of existing political bodies to recognize, as the socialists were prepared to do, the continually increasing importance of the "labour interest" in a country, which, with a maturing capitalist economy and a well-established class system, was now verging on political democracy'.[7] Indeed, the extent to which Labour's ultimate replacement of the Liberals as the major opposition party can be attributed more to the tactical mistakes on the part of the Liberals rather than the simple expansion of the franchise is still a matter of some dispute among historians.[8] Both factors undoubtedly contributed, but it is likely that neither were as important as the growth of the trade unions in making a Labour Party possible.

The new way developed by the ILP socialists has come to be called the doctrine of Labourism. It suggested that 'the only basis for a distinctive political organization of Labour was not Socialism, but quite simply

---

[5] *ibid.*, p. 153.

[6] Barker, B., (ed.), *Ramsay MacDonald's Political Writings*, Allen Lane, 1972, p. 162.

[7] Pelling, H., *The Origins of the Labour Party*, Oxford University Press, 1965, pp. 11–12.

[8] See for example, Chamberlain, C., 'The Growth of Support for the Labour Party in Britain', *British Journal of Sociology*, 1973, vol. XXIV, no. 4.

Labourism'.[9] There is no universally agreed definition of 'Labourism', and more often than not it is used vaguely as a term of abuse. Many writers agree that the concept of 'Labourism' is a useful label which can be applied to a distinctive political idea, although those same writers often disagree about what the idea actually is. Many see Labourism as the simple attachment of socialist intellectuals to the organized but unpoliticized working class. With the help of the intellectuals, Labour Parties therefore become, in the words of Rawson, 'a working class attempt to break into political life from an already established position of some strength in the form of trade unionism'.[10] Lichtheim, on the other hand, argues that Labourism is a distinctive feature of the working class itself: 'The great majority of the British (as of every other) working class was instinctively "Labourist" in the sense of emphasizing its corporate separateness, rather than desiring to remodel society in its own image'.[11] Labourist aims are therefore limited aims, more concerned with improving the social status of the working class within existing society than trying to turn the world upside-down. As Beattie puts it:

> The impetus behind both the ILP and the LRC lay not so much in the support of socialist principles as in the general humanitarian concern for the position of industrial labour and/or the poor in general, and a desire to improve the social status of the working class . . . To such men, the working class was not a 'class' in the Marxist sense; it was a group mainly defined in the (negative) terms of its sense of exclusion from communal life and politics.[12]

Miliband, in his highly influential *Parliamentary Socialism*, uses the term 'Labourism' continually without ever really defining it, but it is clear that he sees it as the voluntary integration of the Labour movement into the parliamentary system. His main thesis is that the Labour Party has been more devoted to the preservation of the parliamentary system than socialism or anything else, and among other things, this slavish adherence to sham debating-floor battles at the expense of the struggle outside parliament has merely served to perpetuate and deepen the already-evident emasculation of the Labour movement.

---

[9] Lichtheim, G., *A Short History of Socialism*, Weidenfeld and Nicolson, 1970, p. 203.

[10] Rawson, D. W., 'The Life Span of Labour Parties', *Political Studies*, 1969, vol. XVII, no. 3, p. 316.

[11] Lichtheim, *op. cit.*, p. 205.

[12] Beattie, A. (ed.), *English Party Politics, Vol. II The Twentieth Century*, Wiedenfeld and Nicolson, 1970, pp. 223–4.

A similar but clearer analysis is provided by Tom Nairn.[13] He sees Labourism as a kind of 'short-cut' or 'second best' socialism, which as we have seen, is a reasonably accurate, if unsympathetic, portrayal of the circumstances surrounding the origin of the LRC. Of the ILP he writes:

> They speedily realized that ... they must either induce the Trade Unions to throw in their lot with them or to be content to build up very slowly a party based on individual membership on the Continental socialist model. As they were not prepared to wait, most of them preferred the shorter cut of a Labour Party based mainly on Trade Union affiliations, even though they realized that they could get such a partly only by a considerable dilution of their socialist objectives ...[14]

Such a party would also have a built-in structural weakness because it would never be capable of mobilizing its predominantly paper membership of less than wholly-committed socialists, a point argued forcefully by the German socialist, Egon Wertheimer, in 1929.[15] A good illustration of the low level of allegiance felt by many trade union affiliated members of the Labour Party occurred in the late forties when the Attlee government repealed the 1927 Trade Union Act. The number of trade union members paying the political levy to the Labour Party (by contracting out rather than in) leapt almost overnight from 2,917,000 to 5,613,000.

On the other hand, such an arrangement has ensured that some kind of socialist party still exists as a major force in British politics, which has not always been the case in some continental countries. But, as Nairn points out, the price has been ideological compromise and the sacrificing of socialist purity. This was fully realized and wholly expected by the originators of Labourism, but Nairn argues that they failed to do much converting to socialism, and instead became passive reflectors of existing working class consciousness as expressed through organizations like the TUC: 'British Trade Unionism could not avoid stifling British Socialism within one unified body, given the immense strength of the former and the weakness and incoherence of the latter'.[16] Moreover, he also argues that the Labourists never really tried to engage in much socialist education and propaganda because they had a mistaken notion that ordinary trade unionists were 'somehow naturally "socialist" in a solid British way'.[17]

---

[13] Nairn, T., 'The Nature of the Labour Party' in Anderson, P. and Blackburn, R. (eds.), *Towards Socialism*, Fontana, 1965, pp. 159–217.

[14] *ibid.*, p. 169.

[15] Wertheimer, E., *Portrait of the Labour Party*, Putnam, 1929.

[16] Nairn, *op. cit.*, p. 188.

[17] *ibid.*, p. 171.

Labourism implied that 'an organization embracing Trade Unionism and Socialism together, and summing-up all the latent might of the working class, *must* be right in principle'. Labourism's relationship to the class it represents is in essence, therefore, a passive one:

> Historically, it accepts the working class and the organizations the latter evolved in its long development, the Trade Unions, as given, decisive facts. Arriving late upon the scene, the organ of a class already profoundly adapted to the conditions of bourgeois society and imbued with its conservatism, it sees its function as no more than a continuation, a further step in this evolution.[18]

At this point we might say that the theory of Labourism would therefore seem to distinguish Labourism from socialism at a number of levels and in terms of a series of polar opposites, which I have summarized in the table below. The characteristics in the left-hand column describe the Labourist 'ideal type' or the 'world-view' of Labourism, while those in the right hand column describe the ideal-typical socialist or socialist 'world-view':

Labourist	Socialist
Passive	Active
Reflexive	Educative
Empirical	Ideological
Pragmatic	Principled
Evolutionary	Revolutionary
Practical	Intellectual
'Ethic of responsibility'	'Ethic of ultimate ends'

Obviously, this list is not exhaustive, nor does it mean that a particular individual cannot exhibit characteristics from both columns. But the distinction between Labourism and Socialism would seem a useful one to make whether applied historically or whether it is used to explain divisions with the contemporary Labour Party or the words and actions of individuals within the national leadership and within local Labour parties.

It might strike the reader that Nairn's account of Labourism and the origins of the Labour Party is somewhat unfair, that the 'short-cut' socialists were not as opportunist, unprincipled, or as stupid as he makes out. Yet, as I have already indicated, to portray the early Labourists as 'opportunists' may be merely to describe what happened, it may not necessarily be inaccurate, nor does it imply that they should be condemned for what

---

[18] *ibid.*, pp. 187, 172.

they did, because, as we have seen, there were very good historical reasons for it. Second, if the 'opportunist' label does imply a critique of the early Labourists, then the evidence and arguments for and against the view that they were excessively unprincipled need to be examined. For instance, Moore has provided an interesting local account of the 'opportunist' nature of early Labourism in his study of four Durham mining villages in the first quarter of the century. After describing how the fledgling Labour Party had an uphill struggle to oust the Liberals from a position of hegemony in the mining communities, Moore concluded that:

> The Labour Party was not, however, concerned to make traditional proletarians out of a population that showed such a large measure of traditional deferentialism. It was trying to win votes. A series of interviews with early Labour organizers, including the Labour electoral agent for the constituency in which most of the villagers voted, showed that Labour in fact compromised with existing social outlooks in order to win votes.[19]

Moore is anxious to dispel other myths, too, like the one about 'the history of the miners being the history of class struggle': 'Far from being in the van of class politics, the miners appear to have been reluctant latecomers. Furthermore the affiliation of the miners to the Labour Party, far from injecting combative class attitudes into the Labour Party, had the opposite effect'.[20] He also argues that the subsequent growth of the Labour Party was aided by fortuitous historical circumstance, and 'perhaps without the intransigience and severity of the coal-owners' demands upon the miners the Labour Party would have failed'.[21]

An earlier study of Labourism at the local level came to similar conclusions. In their analysis of social change in South West Wales, Brennan and colleagues examined the relationship between the early Labour Party and the chapels.[22] They found that much early socialist 'preaching' had a distinctly 'religious' flavour, and this was apparently designed to woo the chapel vote. The need to pursue such an apparently compromising strategy receded rapidly after the First World War, but this was not due to the

---

[19] Moore, R. S., 'Religion as a Source of Variation in Working Class Images of Society', in *Proceedings of the Social Science Research Council Conference: The Occupational Community of the Traditional Worker*, Durham, 1973.

[20] *ibid.*, p. 39.

[21] *ibid.*, p. 66.

[22] Brennan, T., Cooney, E. W., and Pollins, H., *Social Change in South West Wales*, Watts, 1954, esp. p. 148.

strength of socialist ideology *per se*. Rather, they argue, it could be explained by the deteriorating economic situation, successive economic and political crises, and the attitude of the coal-owners, who were not exactly practising the 'brotherhood of man' advocated by the chapels. It was this combination of circumstances which radicalized the working class in South West Wales, and not the Labour Party, although the latter was to gain in the process.

Another factor which undoubtedly assisted the early growth of the Labour Party was the favourable attitude of some industrialists. As Williams pointed out, Labourism was actually welcomed by enlightened capitalists such as the Cadbury family for reasons to do with the creation of a 'happier' (capitalist) community, because a healthier, happier work-force is a more efficient work-force.[23] Others welcomed Labourism as the best possible alternative to revolution, a kind of insurance policy against full-blooded socialism. In this way they were at one with Joseph Chamberlain who had elucidated earlier his concept of the 'Gospel of Ransom' which involved 'the payment in social services and improved working conditions of the sum necessary to avoid the danger of revolution'.[24] In fact, this very argument was also used in Fabian propaganda, much of which was specifically aimed at sections of the ruling class rather than the working class.

There was a distinctive 'Britishness' about Labourism which really needs emphasizing, and this could be seen at various levels. For example, Guttsman is one of the many writers who have been particularly interested in the process by which Labour Party leaders readily adopted a concept of leadership which largely assimilated the attitudes traditionally held by the representatives of other British political parties.[25] But by far the most interesting description of the essentially 'British' character of the Labour Party is contained in Egon Wertheimer's 1929 *Portrait of the Labour Party*. 'The close connection of British Labour with British national culture and tradition' provides the main theme, which he develops by contrasting the characteristics of British Socialism with its continental counterparts. For instance, on 'cultural' questions like morality and sexual equality, he shows that the British Labour Party was entirely conventional.[26]

This is mainly because it was never intended that the Labour Party should represent a clean break with the British political culture. As we have

---

[23] Williams, *op. cit.*, p. 145.

[24] *ibid.*, p. 83.

[25] Guttsman, W. L., *The British Political Elite*, MacGibbon and Kee, 1963, ch. IX.

[26] Wertheimer, *op. cit.*, pp. 90–1.

already seen, the Labour Party itself 'did not come into being in response to any theory about what a Socialist party should be; it arose empirically, in a quite piecemeal fashion, like so much in British bourgeois society before it'.[27] Just as the British political culture has been characterized by empiricism, compromise, deference, stability and evolutionism, so was the new Labour Party. The other reason why the Labour Party conformed to the norms and traditions of the British political culture was that it had to in order to win votes, evident in the local studies of Wales and Durham. If it did not win votes, then there seemed little point in having a Labour Party, because a Labour Party was there to get candidates 'sympathetic to the aims of the Labour movement' elected to parliament.

Winning votes involved compromises, but, as the Labour Party grew, too many compromises would serve to alienate the rank and file activists, so Labour leaders had to steer a delicate middle course expressing 'the need to move onwards from denunciation without losing in the process the fire and enthusiasm that sustained it earlier'.[28] In fact, there was a great deal of disillusionment with the parliamentary impact of Labour, a feeling that high hopes had not been fulfilled, right up until the First World War, and this, some say, led eventually to Hardie's resignation as Chairman of the PLP. In particular, the lack of a clearly-defined policy, the limitations imposed by parliamentary democracy, and the predilection of Labour leaders for electoral deals with the Liberals did little to enthuse trade unionists and the Labour rank and file. Had the First World War not come along with its disastrous repercussions, it is likely that Labour would have remained an insignificant minority party for many years.

Labourism's adherence to the empiricist and evolutionary traditions of the British political culture was partly mediated through the Fabians and special mention should be made of their role as the 'intellectuals' of the Labour movement. An exclusively middle class group of 'thinkers', the Fabian Society was founded in 1883. They took their name from the Roman general Fabius Cunctator, who was apparently renowned for his cautious military philosophy, and they adopted the motto: 'For the right moment you must wait, as Fabius did most patiently, when warring against Hannibal, though many censured his delays; but when the time comes you must strike hard, as Fabius did, or your waiting will be in vain, and fruitless'. Lichtheim says that there is no record of when Fabius 'struck hard', and:

---

[27] Nairn, *op. cit.*, p. 159.
[28] Williams, *op. cit.*, p. 161.

malicious critics of Fabianism have been known to hint that there may have been something prophetic, or at least symbolic, in this misreading of history and that anyone who expects Fabians to 'strike hard' for Socialism or anything else is quite likely to have to wait until Doomsday. Be that as it may, the Society from the start was committed to taking the long view.[29]

That long view saw history as a gradual process of evolution towards a better society. It was not concerned with fighting the class war, or creating social revolution and abolishing capitalism, but with creating the conditions for gradual, peaceful reform by winning over the middle classes and the ruling class through the moral force and economic sense of their arguments. But it was their emphasis on economics, more particularly the detailed working-out of state-run welfare schemes and plans for state intervention in the economy which contributed so much to the empirical and economistic approach of Labourism. It also earned them the nick-name of the 'Institute of Social Engineering'. Fabianism therefore provided a kind of non-intellectual intellectual dimension to Labourism. The empiricism and economism of the Labour movement, the lack of interest in ideologies and wordly philosophies was reflected in, and complemented by, the social engineering of Fabian technicians.

That Fabianism and Labourism reflected the traditions of the British political culture is certainly interesting and useful. Though something of a truism, in that the reception accorded to any world wide ideology (like socialism) is bound to be dependent on the conditions prevailing in each particular country, it contributes something to our understanding of the phenomenon that is the Labour Party.[30] It may also help us choose between the competing traditions of what I called the 'History of Glorious Struggle' and 'History of Betrayal'. But it doesn't help us answer some of the larger questions unless we extend the analysis and fill in the gaps. Situating Labourism is all very well, but alone it doesn't allow us to grasp the essence of what the Labour Party is all about.

We have already explained how some have seen the Labour Party, among other things, as an essentially passive receptacle of existing working class opinion and values. This implies that the Labour Party was not really out to change society radically and abruptly by winning active mass sup-

[29] Lichtheim, *op. cit.*, p. 190.
[30] It should be noted, however, that the very concept of 'political culture' is somewhat controversial, and should be treated with circumspection. It is, for instance, misleading to see it as a static, rather than dynamic entity.

port, but merely to facilitate society's evolution in a progressive direction, with the help of working class votes at election time. The question therefore arises: to what extent did the Labour Party make history and to what extent was it made by history? Was the Labour Party born through 'struggle' or did it just 'happen'? Such questions are virtually impossible to answer fully, but the analysis of Labourism presented here would seem to support the view that the Labour Party was created by history rather than its creator. Like the Unions, it is reflected in its origins and early evolution as an essentially defensive organization. Without Taff Vale and the Osborne Judgement, for example, the fledgling Labour Party would not have gained Union support as quickly as it did. Without the First World War and the extension of the franchise, Labour would not have grown so rapidly in the early 1920s. Without the Second World War, Labour would not have had its great historical opportunity in 1945. There is, therefore, a sense in which the Labour Party itself is irrelevant to the total process of social change. It is a medium or instrument through which social change occurs, not its origin. Even Francis Williams, whose 'History of Glorious Struggle' has been quoted above, is forced to admit this in places. He begins his eminently readable history of the Labour Party by suggesting that the decision to found the LRC 'was to mobilize behind it and become the chief instrument of a political uprising of the working classes of Britain that was to change the social and economic face of the country out of all recognition.'[31] But towards the end of the book he is saying:

> The nearly 4,350,000 electors who voted for Labour in 1924 were brought to a belief in Labour policy not simply by successful propaganda, but by the harsh logic of events. The Labour Party was – and was to continue to be – not the creator of a social and economic revolution, but its instrument. Its growing strength was due to the manifest fact that whatever successes the old economic system had been able to claim in the past, it was not adequate to deal with the economic problems that now pressed upon Britain with such implacable force.[32]

History also determined, to a great extent, the *content* of Labour's programmes and policies. To a party concerned with achieving a parliamentary majority by winning votes, the 'mood of the voters' was, and is, the primary consideration. In this respect, the British experience of two

[31] Williams, *op. cit.*, p. 9.
[32] *ibid.*, pp. 287–8.

major wars and a severe economic depression in the space of thirty years was of paramount importance. As Bealey points out:

> The mood of the voters, conditioned by two world wars and inter-war depression, has been towards *security rather than adventure*. Consequently, visionary and ethical socialism, characteristic of the early years, has had less and less impact; and since the passage of the nationalization measures twenty years ago, there has been a natural tendency to concentrate on the practical problems of public ownership. It was not the socialist theoreticians, but the technocrats of the mixed economy who ultimately most affected the Party's official thinking.[33]

One key to understanding the Labour Party is to examine the historical role of ideology in the Labour Party, especially the role of socialist ideology. In this next section, we shall look at the relationship between the Labour Party and socialism, and attempt an assessment of the extent to which the Labour Party can now be, or could have been regarded in the past to be 'socialist'. Has there been a 'de-radicalization' of the Labour Party? Has socialism been betrayed by successive Labour leaderships or was it always an illusion, a symbolic 'myth'?

The Labour Party and Socialism

> The International Bureau declares that the British Labour Party be permitted to attend International Socialist Congresses as, although it does not directly recognize the proletarian class struggle, it nevertheless wages the struggle and in fact and by its very organization, which is independent of the bourgeois parties, is adopting the basis of the class struggle.[34]

We noted above that the Labour Party only came about after other socialist groups had failed. They had been unable to make major ideological inroads into the traditional deference and material preoccupations of working class people. Shaw Desmond, a former ILP soap-box orator, gave a vivid account of the kind of problems they were up against in his *Labour: The Giant With the Feet of Clay*, published in 1921.[35] For

---

[33] Bealey, F. (ed.), *The Social and Political Thought of The Labour Party*, Weidenfeld and Nicolson, 1970, p. 51.

[34] Lenin, V. I., in 'The Session of the International Socialist Bureau' (of the 2nd International), *Lenin on Britain*, Lawrence and Wishart, 1934, pp. 93–8 (with an introduction by Harry Pollitt).

[35] Desmond, S., *Labour: The Giant with the Feet of Clay*, Collins, 1921.

example, he cites Robert Blatchford, author of *Merrie England* as saying: 'The thing that was troubling the factory girl was not either the downtrodden proletariat or the theory behind International Socialism, but what she was going to put in her stomach and what the Duke said to the Duchess in the conservatory after dinner.'[36] He also quotes a 'former respected Labour leader' as saying: 'Of course Labour must develop its machine. We shall never be able to make conscious socialists of more than a small minority.'[37]

An influential minority of socialist delegates at the Founding Conference of the LRC accepted this argument too, and they joined with the non-socialist majority in rejecting a clear commitment to the socialist class struggle. Apart from not wanting to alienate other non-socialist trade unionists, some believed that a clear commitment to socialism at that stage would condemn them to perpetual obscurity like the other socialist groupings. But the varying strength of the socialist, non-socialist, and pragmatic factions in the LRC produced some confusing results. For instance, from LRC and early Labour Party conference reports, McKenzie shows how similar motions on the overthrow of capitalism and the public ownership of the means of production were narrowly defeated in 1903, passed *nem con* in 1905, rejected overwhelmingly in 1907, and passed again in 1908, though usually as ordinary resolutions rather than constitutional amendments.[38] Other modern scholars, too, have been keen to correct what they see as a mistaken impression that socialist principles played a large part in the early history of the Labour Party. Beattie, for instance, argues that the Labour Party has always been less explicable in terms of socialist ideology than many have suggested.[39] Former Labour leaders in particular have frequently overstated the role of socialist principles.

In fact, 'socialism', was not adopted by the Labour Party as its ultimate goal until 1918. In that year, the Annual Conference approved a new constitution based on Sidney and Beatrice Webb's Fabian policy document 'Labour and the New Social Order'. Among other things, the constitution included for the first time the famous Clause IV. But more than one author has argued that this new commitment to socialism came about, not

---

[36] *ibid.*, p. 38.

[37] *ibid.*, p. 64.

[38] McKenzie, R. T., *British Political Parties: The Distribution of Power Within the Conservative and Labour Parties*, Heinemann, 1963 (2nd edn.), p. 387 and pp. 465–6.

[39] Beattie, A. (ed.), *op. cit.*, p. 221. See also Bealey, F. and Pelling, H., *Labour and Politics 1900–1906: A History of the Labour Representation Committee*, MacMillan, 1958; and Pelling, H., *A Short History of the Labour Party*, MacMillan, 1972 (4th edn.).

through any sudden ideological conversion, but through a pragmatic realization by the minority Labour Party that (a) new policies and ideas were needed to solve the economic problems of capitalism, and (b) it would need to clearly differentiate itself from the other major political parties if it wanted to achieve similar prominence as an alternative government party. Put rather more crudely, Labour would have to come up with some new idea, theme or gimmick if it was to get anywhere, and capitalize on the millions of new working class votes.

This argument is most closely associated with Samuel H. Beer, whose *Modern British Politics* is a familiar text for many students. He says that 'the adoption of Socialism set the seal on the decision of 1900 to form a separate and independent political party'.[40] The trade unions' experience of war-time state intervention, pressure from committed socialists within the Party, the difficulty of remaining independent whilst working with the Liberals, and above all, the real possibility of achieving parliamentary power with the help of the new working class votes, convinced the Labour leadership that a serious, independent bid for power was no longer within the realms of fantasy:

> The adoption of Socialism as an ideology was functional to this choice of political independence. If the party was to pursue power independently, it needed a set of beliefs and values distinguishing it from other parties. For the sake of its own followers, present and prospective, the party had to articulate in its declaration of purpose the profound sense of difference – or, if you like, alienation – that sprang from their consciousness of class. ... One can only agree with the wisdom of Arthur Henderson when he concluded in 1917 that 'some sort of Socialist faith was the necessary basis for the consolidation of the Labour Party into an effective national force'.[41]

Beer therefore sees socialism as a kind of rationalization of the thrust for power, but also something which provided the activists and supporters with a sense of common purpose, it instilled a certain amount of pride and confidence in class, and held out the promise of a better society. But, as an ominous footnote he adds:

> If this analysis of the decisions of 1918 is correct, it raises various interesting suggestions about the later history of the Labour Party. One is

---

[40] Beer, S. H., *Modern British Politics: A Study of Parties and Pressure Groups*, Faber, 1969 (2nd edn.), p. 140.

[41] *ibid.*, pp. 149–50.

the possibility that if the thrust for power was the main driving force behind the adoption of Socialism, it might be expected that when and as power was won by organized Labour, the concern with Socialist ideology would decline.[42]

Except that power would have to be won again, and support would need to be mobilized at the next election.

The main problem with this kind of analysis is that it is, in certain senses, unanswerable. To argue that the adoption of socialism was 'functional' to the Labour Party, is, in one sense, stating the obvious since everything is 'functional'. It is an easy panacea for 'explaning' why something is as it is. In another sense, too, it is impossible to disprove because the Labour Party did indeed adopt socialism and not something else. But if the argument is that the Labour leaders at the time cynically chose socialism out of mere political expediency rather than anything else, then this is a matter for historians to test in relation to available facts.

Certainly there is evidence which supports Beer's case. For instance, statements made at the 1918 and subsequent Annual Conferences are indicative of just how serious some distinguished Labour persons were about socialism. In fact, at the 1918 conference, in the very first discussion impinging on Clause IV of the newly-adopted Constitution, conference chairman Sidney Webb informed delegates that 'they did not want repeatedly, over and over again, to ring the changes on the old shibboleths'.[43]

Now the dictionary says that 'shibboleth' means the 'watchword of a party', a 'party cry' or the 'pet-phrase of a party', and this is precisely what some have argued socialism is to the Labour party – a pet phrase. Richard Crossman, no less, writing in *Encounter* in 1954, stated that socialism was viewed by most European socialist leaders as a 'Utopian myth ... often remote from the realities of day-to-day politics'. He continued:

A democratic party can very rarely be persuaded to give up one of its central principles, and can never afford to scrap its central myth. Conservatives must defend free enterprise even when they are actually introducing state planning. A Labour government must defend as true Socialism policies which have very little to do with it. The job of the party leaders is often to persuade their followers that the traditional policy is still being carried out, even when this is demonstrably not true.[44]

---

[42] *ibid.*, p. 152.

[43] See Nairn, *op. cit.*, p. 184, and the 1918 Annual Conference Report, pp. 44 ff and p. 64.

[44] Crossman, R. H. S., 'On Political Neurosis', *Encounter*, May 1954, no. 3, pp. 66–7.

While Crossman had described the role of what he called 'myth' in parties and the political process, the French political scientist Maurice Duverger preferred to call it the phenomenon of 'camouflage', a concept which he applied to all parties, classes and groups, and to the individual members, not just the leaders:

> The image that a party, class or a group projects of itself is an idealized image, like that of a product praised by advertising; idealization is a means of attracting customers, or supporters, of fighting a competitor or an opponent . . . every ideology tends to give its followers a rather glorified image of themselves, one they can contemplate with satisfaction. Frequently, there is only a partial awareness of the deception.[45]

But in relation to the Labour Party, as long ago as 1921, Shaw Desmond in the remarkable book quoted above, likened the 'myth' of socialism in the Labour Party to Christianity's promise for the future.[46]

In a similar way, the conflict between the teachings of Christ and the every-day actions and behaviour of Christians has been likened to the conflict in the Labour Party between long term aspirations and the Party's performance in office.[47] In this respect, therefore, the role of 'myth' or 'camouflage' is to provide a long term aim, to generate a sense of common purpose sufficient to motivate the party faithful, and to unite the disparate elements of the party into one cohesive national organization. Subsequent periodic bouts of disillusionment there will be, but, says Saville,

> . . . in the Labour Movement, memories of past follies of Labour administrations have had plenty of time to fade and grow dim, before the next shock is administered. Myths and illusions form an interesting and often an extraordinary part of the political behaviour of many individuals who make up the Labour movement. If this were not so, the cultivation of private gardens would perhaps be carried on even more rigorously than is already the case.[48]

Part of the argument of Hindess and others is that there has indeed been an increase in 'the cultivation of private gardens', a decline in participation in the Labour movement.

---

[45] Duverger, M., *The Study of Politics* (trans. R. Wagoner), Nelson, 1972.

[46] Desmond, *op. cit.*, p. 192.

[47] Jarman, T. L., *Socialism in Britain*, Gollancz, 1972, p. 134.

[48] Saville, J., 'Labourism and the Labour Government', in *Socialist Register 1967*, Merlin Press, 1967, p. 44.

The kind of 'socialism' adopted by the Labour Party in 1918 was based on the evolutionary theories of the Fabians – meritocratic rather than egalitarian, evolutionary rather than revolutionary and dedicated to class conciliation rather than class struggle. Miliband described the contents of 'Labour and the New Social Order' as follows: 'Shorn of its rhetoric' it was 'a Fabian blueprint for a more advanced, more regulated form of Capitalism'.[49] But the overall approach to the social system had been laid down earlier in, among other places, the copious writings of that highly-influential but now much-neglected figure of the Labour Party, Ramsay MacDonald. In *Socialism and Society* (1905), the future Labour Prime Minister wrote: 'Socialism marks the growth of society, not the uprising of a class. The consciousness which it seeks to quicken is not one of economic class solidarity, but one of social unity and growth towards organic wholeness.'[50] And later:

> This completeness of organisation, this idea of national and communal growth, this state of business efficiency, nothing short of it and nothing which is sectional in it, should be laid down as the basis of Socialism. And the political movement . . . must be a movement of the whole of society and not one of its functions – the working class.[51]

A major task, therefore, was the win over the middle class to the 'intellectual proposals' of socialism. Two years later, he presented a similar version of socialism, this time clearly differentiating it from that of the 'fully fledged Socialists':

> . . . it is practically impossible to maintain a pure and simple Socialist Party . . . In Great Britain at present, political parties are in confusion, but the lines of division between two great parties are emerging. The mass of the people are prepared to accept the new doctrines not as absolute ideas, as the fully fledged Socialists do, but as guiding principles in experimental legislation. That is what the rise of the Labour Party means – that is all it ever need mean, because that is how society develops from stage to stage in its existence.[52]

Now there were, of course, many people at the time who thought that the rise of the Labour Party meant something more than that. And many today would certainly dispute MacDonald's version of how society works and

---

[49] Miliband, *Parliamentary Socialism, op. cit.*, p. 62.

[50] See Barker, *Ramsay MacDonald's Political Writings, op. cit.*, p. 93.

[51] *ibid.*, p. 95.

[52] *ibid.*, p. 161.

how it develops. But that is not the point. What matters is that these kinds of ideas and conceptions of socialism existed, gained wide currency and were frequently articulated by important Labour leaders in those crucially formative years of the early Labour Party. We can still see their influence today in Labour Party thinking.[53]

But what *is* Labour Party thinking? Has there been a coherent body of ideas which could be called Labour Party 'thought'? From the start the LRC carefully avoided a clear programme for various reasons, and detailed policy making was left to the PLP. There have indeed been political programmes adopted from time to time, there has always been the 'shibboleth' of Clause IV, and the basic approach of Labourism has remained the same, but there has been no coherent body of ideas, analysis of society, or defined programme which one could point to at any time in the last 50 years and say: *that* is 'what the Labour Party stands for'. In fact, one comparatively recent author, in a propagandist work designed to woo the 'floating voter', experienced great difficulty in explaining precisely what Labour stood for and how it differed from the Tories. All he could say was that there were 'fundamental' differences between the parties, even though they were 'broadly agreed' on some things and some differences were 'exaggerated in disputes'.[54] It is also possible to point to different Labour leaders and thinkers putting forward the most diverse and contradictory ideas at different times, wholly at variance in terms of their ideological basis.[55]

In reality, Labour Party thinking as a whole has always proceeded empirically, advancing, then stumbling, reacting and trimming. Events, ideas, experiences, personalities and electoral possibilities have all played their part, though the development of Labour Party thinking has been loaded in the long run by the condition and evolution of the national economy, and

---

[53] See, for instance, Jenkins, R., *What Matters Now* (Fontana, 1972, p. 22): 'Nor can we trust to class loyalties of the traditional kind: the gulf between majority and minority now cuts across class lines. Our only hope is to appeal to the latent idealism of all men and women of goodwill – irrespective of their income brackets, irrespective of their class origins, irrespective in many cases of their past political affiliations'. And p. 118: '. . . an appeal to class interest and class emotion is incompatible with the vision of a classless society which has always been one of the chief inspirations of democratic socialism'.

[54] Northcott, J., *Why Labour?*, Penguin, 1964, p. 12.

[55] R. I. McKibbin, in a D.Phil. thesis (Oxford, 1970), makes the interesting point that after the adoption of 'socialism' in 1918 'The Labour Party had a socialist objective but not a socialist ideology; service to the Movement and service to the Labour Party's organization as the political expression of the Movement became an alternative ideology'. It can be seen that the ideology of 'service' to the movement became more significant as the Labour Party became more established as a permanent fixture in national party politics. See footnote p. 72.

he nature of the system of power relations which has constituted the Par-
y's universe.

There are really two levels at which we can examine the evolution of
Labour Party thought. The first, the explicit, involves looking at the
policies and specific programmes which have emerged and evolved. For
example, it might be shown how the publication of Douglas Jay's *The
Socialist Case* in 1937 marked a turning point in Labour Party thinking
way from nationalization towards the redistribution of incomes. The se-
ond, the implicit, involves looking at the assumptions behind the policies,
and the way that Labour Party thought fits into an analysis of 'value
ystems'.

At the first level, Bealey provides a brief commentary on the actual
development of Labour Party thought in his introduction to *The Social
and Political Thought of the British Labour Party*.[56] He suggests that
Labour Party ideas and policies have varied over the years under the in-
luence of three key factors. First of these was the proximity of the Labour
Party to power. He argues that it was more concerned with fundamental
values in its early days, but became more and more pre-occupied with finding solutions to specific problems as it became closer to actually forming a
overnment. Second, and perhaps most important, the state of the
conomy conditioned both the Labour Party and the trade unions' attitude
to social questions of the day. And third, events in other countries proved
highly influential. As to the overall direction of Labour thought in the
wentieth century, Bealey sees it as being one long ideological decline from
1918 to the present day whereby 'pragmatism had asserted itself at all
evels'.[57] He says that party thinking has become more technical, academic
and voter-orientated: there has been a 'growing insistence of the efficiency
of leadership rather than dedication to doctrine' and an 'increasing faith in
public relations rather than grass roots contact'.[58]

There is little doubt that many people would accept this intuitively as
being correct, that these are two senses in which there has indeed been a
decline of working class politics'. But both propositions are extremely
dubious. There is, it is true, very little attention given to doctrine and the
development of socialist thought by most contemporary Labour leaders,
and one could enumerate the reasons why this is so.[59] My point is that this

---

[56] Bealey, *op. cit.*, pp. 1–54.
[57] *ibid.*, p. 49.
[58] *ibid.*, pp. 52–3.
[59] Coates, *op. cit.*, pp. 145–6. See also Hall, P., *Labour's New Frontiers*, Deutsch, 1964, p. 2.

has always been the case, and 'dedication to doctrine' has always run a poor second to 'efficiency of leadership'. This is all the more obvious the more one explores the speeches and actions of early Labour leaders, and the Annual Conference reports. Ramsay MacDonald may indeed have written at length about his version of socialism, and his thoughts may indeed have been influential, but socialist doctrine itself never figured greatly in the everyday actions of Labour leaders.

Similarly, it is certainly true that 'grass-roots contact' in local working class communities has become almost totally overshadowed by London-organized, TV-orientated, public relations efforts, a phenomenon common to all political parties and pressure groups. But this does not mean to say that the fabled 'grass roots contact' was really any more significant in the past than it is today. As we shall see in the next chapter, there really is very little evidence to support any assertion that there has been a significant decline in local Labour Party activity measured over the last forty or fifty years.

Moreover, it is clear from the account of the origins of Labourism that the Labour Party has always been pragmatic in approach, often technical and academic in its economic and social thinking, and certainly very 'voter-orientated'. To suggest otherwise, to imply that this is a new development, is misleading.

At the second level of analysis, one can look in more general terms at the values underlying Labour Party thought, and in this context, Parkin has put forward an interesting schema: he argues that it is possible to distinguish three different sets of values or value systems in Britain which are attributable to different sections of society, depending upon whether that section or class is dominant, subordinate or radical.[60] The 'dominant value system' is the set of values held by the dominant class, defining for them what is self-evidently 'right' or 'good'. Essentially it sees society as an organic unity, with a strong emphasis on the interests of 'the Nation'. Members of the subordinate class who hold similar values are held to be 'deferential' towards their natural superiors in the dominant class. Second, the 'subordinate value system', says Parkin, is based on the working class community and is essentially accommodative of the social system. It neither endorses the present social arrangements nor violently opposes them. Third, the 'radical value system' embraces traditional class-orientated radical thinking. Rather than encouraging consciousness of national identity or consciousness of the local community, the 'radical

---

[60] Parkin, *op. cit.*, ch. 3.

value system' promotes consciousness of class, and, says Parkin, its very survival as a way of thinking against the pressures of 'dominant' and subordinate' thinking is largely dependent on the continued espousal of radical class-based ideology by the mass party of the working class.

This is where the Labour Party comes in. For it is abundantly clear that Labour Party thought has included elements of radical, subordinate and dominant values. But, says Parkin, if the radical value system is to gain ground at the expense of others, if radical change is to occur, it needs to be constantly nourished, especially by an effective educational effort by the leadership of the mass working class party, the Labour Party. In common with the authors of the May Day manifesto and the Cambridge 'Affluent Worker' studies, Parkin concludes that the Labour Party has a potentially more formative influence on the political perceptions and understandings of the subordinate class than is generally acknowledged:

> Once established among the subordinate class, the radical mass party is able to provide its supporters with political cues, signals and information of a very different kind from those made available by the dominant culture. To a considerable degree, workers may look to their Party for political guidance in an attempt to make sense of their social world.[61]

Yet the Labour Party has never fully adhered to the 'radical value system' or fully accepted this alleged formative influence, and a number of writers have pointed out that it has never consciously set out to create and sustain a radical or proletarian sub-culture in opposition to the dominant capitalist culture.[62] As Anderson puts it, the British Labour Party, unlike other Continental mass parties (especially the communist parties), has never been a 'hegemonic' party, providing its supporters with an all-embracing ideology and determining their whole way of life. Nor has its aim been primarily to make 'converts' to its 'cause' — socialism.[63] This quasi-passive reflection of 'subordinate' working class attitudes and beliefs with very little serious effort to transform 'subordinate' attitudes into 'radical' attitudes is one of the hallmarks of Labourism.

---

[61] *ibid.*, p. 99.

[62] See Wertheimer, *op. cit.*; also Nairn, *op. cit.*, p. 175.

[63] Anderson, 'Problems of Socialist Strategy', in Anderson, P. and Blackburn, R. (eds.), *Towards Socialism*, Fontana, 1965, pp. 237 ff; also Miliband, *op. cit.*, p. 349. Unlike today, the need to make 'converts' to socialism has indeed been stressed at times in the past (see, for instance, the concluding chapter of Attlee, C. R., *The Labour Party in Perspective*, Gollancz, 1937, and items like *Why Vote Labour?* by 'Licinius' (also published by Gollancz in 1945) but it has neither been the prime concern of Labour leaders or constituency activists, nor has it been reflected in practice.

I have attempted in this chapter to convey something of the origins and character of the Labour Party, and to explain how the relationship between the Labour Party and socialism is at once more equivocal and complicated than many would have us believe. But for a fuller understanding of the Labour Party we must go further than that. In the following section I want to look in more detail at various problems connected with the structure of the Labour Party, and also examine various accounts of the overall functions of the Labour Party.

The Labour Party: How it works, What it Does

That the Labour Party has always been a reformist rather than revolutionary organization is beyond doubt. The Labour Representation Committee was founded by elements in the Trade Union movement with the aid of socialist intellectuals. Their initial and essential aim was a simple, vague, reformist one – to improve the lot of the working classes. In order to do this, they felt that they had to gain some measure of parliamentary representation, and this was facilitated in the early days by arranging electoral pacts with the Liberals. But the influence of the Trade Unions in the early growth of the Labour Party – both nationally and locally – cannot be overestimated. Not only did they provide the strength of numbers and finance, but existing Trade Union thinking determined the rate at which the Labour Party would progress to a fully-fledged national, and later 'socialist', party. It is interesting to note that Trade Union interest in the Labour Party rapidly increased after Taff Vale and the Osborne Judgement, both cases where Trade Union rights were challenged by the government of the day. It is this that led authors like Williams, McKenzie and Nairn to conclude that the Labour Party was originally a 'defensive' rather than 'aggressive' organization, brought about to defend the emergent and insufficiently recognized labour interest.

Williams suggests that the ruling class attack of Taff Vale (1901) made a genuine Labour party possible within five years rather than ten or more.[6] McKenzie argues that the Labour Party was 'propelled' into politics, and had the established parties become more sympathetic to the interests of labour, the Labour Party may never have occurred, at least not for a long while.[65] Certainly there is truth in this, but to say that the Labour Party

[64] Williams, *op. cit.*, pp. 139–40.
[65] McKenzie, *op. cit.*, ch. VII.

was 'propelled' into politics is too determinist, and dismissive of the efforts of those who worked for years to bring a Labour party about. Nairn goes further and relates the defensive character of the Labour Party to the state of the British economy and the decline of British Imperialism: 'a long and grim rearguard action was to constitute the universe of the Labour Party. It inherited a declining world . . .'.[66]

These kinds of argument are difficult if not impossible to resolve, but what is clear is that the emergent Labour Party – mostly influenced by the reticent Trade Unions – had very limited aims. According to the LRC Founding Conference, these aims lay in 'securing a better representation of the interests of labour in the House of Commons' and in 'promoting legislation in the direct interest of Labour'. The prospect of actually forming a Government seemed wholly remote and was not seriously discussed until 1918.

Parliament, therefore, from the very beginning provided the main focus of efforts in the labour interest, even to the extent of defending the institution itself against its enemies – like the advocates of 'syndicalism' and 'direct action'. As Miliband – whose book *Parliamentary Socialism* is largely an elaboration of this theme – pointed out, 'the leaders of the Labour Party have always rejected any kind of political action (such as industrial action for political purposes) which fell, or which appeared to fall outside the framework and conventions of the Parliamentary system'.[67] Elsewhere he argues that the Labour Party became rapidly integrated into parliamentary politics just as the modern Trade Unions became more integrated into the State, but this contention is a little difficult to sustain because the Labour Party in its very origins was already integrated into parliamentary politics.

In order to achieve parliamentary labour representation the Labour Party had to win elections. The initial decision of the LRC to concentrate on parliament meant that the primary focus of LRC and early Labour Party activity was in getting Labour 'Lib-Lab', or even sympathetic Liberal candidates elected to parliament to promote legislation 'in the direct interest of labour'. One consequence was that local organizations would be needed for the purpose of conducting election campaigns in the constituencies. It also meant that official Labour candidates usually preferred to modify or trim their policies and the content of their speeches so as not to scare off potential voters. In the absence of a widespread and successful political educa-

---

[66] Nairn, 'The Fateful Meridian', *New Left Review*, 1970, no. 60, p. 4.
[67] Miliband, *op. cit.*, p. 13.

tion effort, Labour candidates would have to compromise in order to convince the 'middle ground' of the electorate that they were 'moderate men'.

The emphasis on elections brought problems too, problems which are every bit as relevant today. One is that concentration on electoral organization inevitably leads to the neglect of political education and mobilization between elections. As Anderson points out:

> By devoting all its energies to the single moment of the vote, the Labour Party necessarily suffers precisely at the vote – since it has neglected to build a more durable community which alone could create the basis for solid and habitual victory at the polls. Electoral success can only come into the bargain, as a consequence of much more fundamental work of education and communication between party and society.

He argues that 'the Labour Party will never be able to unify the working class – or indeed any social group – behind it, as long as it tries to do so through the essentially isolating electoral mechanism.'[68]

Second, concentration on elections, or as some have put it, 'electionism', would be more useful if it weren't for the fact that elections aren't that important in the total process of social change. Social change occurs in many important ways – through the evolution of the national economy and other fundamental processes – which often have little to do with elections and periodic changes in Government. As Dowse and Hughes concluded after an examination of the role of elections in the political process:

> A major implication of this section on elections and the political order is that, by themselves, elections have very little direct influence on the policy and decision-making of Government. Probably of more importance are such things as the pressures which the parties and the groups are likely to exert continuously, the politician's own preferences, external factors such as the state of the economy and foreign relations, prudential consideration, and so on. Perhaps it is the case that elections do have a central place in the democratic credo, but it is not easy to justify this central place empirically.[69]

Once again, a radical party seriously in the business of creating progressive social change cannot afford to rely solely on fighting elections as a means of gaining control of the means of legislation, or to rely solely on control of the means of legislation to bring about change.

---

[68] Anderson, *op. cit.*, p. 256.
[69] Dowse, R. E. and Hughes, J. A., *Political Sociology*, Wiley, 1972, p. 335.

Third, the fact that elections do occupy a central place in the 'democratic credo' means that they inevitably contain a strong ritualistic element, but like other rituals, they often come to have very little meaning for the participants. Voting becomes a chore, a gesture to placate the knocker-up on election night. A party of radical change, a significant proportion of whose supporters fail to voluntarily turn out, but need to be *dug out* on election day, is not a party which has an impressive mandate for radical legislative reform. If it ever wishes to introduce radical socialist measures, it may be unable to appeal successfully for mass support of a non-electoral kind.

Finally, there is the critique of bourgeois or liberal democracy itself. One argument is that the universal franchise or 'one man – one vote' – 'democracy' as we know it – does not confer political equality at all because people are unequal in other ways. As Parkin put it: 'Political equality presupposes sufficient social and material equality to enable contending groups to utilize formal political rights in roughly the same degree. Where sharp social and material inequalities do exist, the provision of equal political rights in effect confers a major advantage on those who command the greatest resources to mobilize in defence of their interests.'[70] Again the implication for the radical party is that it must not overestimate the importance of an 'egalitarian' political order where a profoundly inegalitarian social and economic order exists.

Party organization – in the technical sense – has always been a problem for Labour. But the precise status and functions of the party outside parliament has always been, and continues to be, a source of controversy. The very decision to re-constitute the LRC as a political 'party', fighting elections, running candidates for parliament, meant that Labour would require an electoral machine capable of equalling – and beating – the Tories and Liberals at their own game. This meant the setting up of local organizations of the party – first accepted tentatively on a federal basis in 1905, but not fully embraced until 1918 – which would mainly function as electioneering bodies. But there are many who would disagree with this analysis. They would argue that Labour's grass-roots organizations are, or at least are supposed to be more than that, that they are part of an overall democratic Labour 'movement' which embraces the Unions and the local constituency parties, as well as the Parliamentary Labour Party, representatives of whom all meet once a year to hammer-out Labour Party policy at the Annual Conference or 'parliament' of the 'movement'.

---

[70] Parkin, *op. cit.*, p. 185.

Others argue that, for all practical purposes, the Labour Party is really the Parliamentary Party, and the local organizations are no more than electoral machines (and inefficient ones at that), with no real power or say in the running of the party, either through annual conferences, regional conferences, or anything else. Of course the PLP leadership cannot ignore the wishes of the activists who do the work in the constituencies, but they are not bound to accept their advice and can pretty much do as they please, provided they can keep the local activists reasonably happy and contented by convincing them that everything they do is another step towards socialism. Which view provides the more accurate picture of the true position?

The Labour Party is a political party, and as such is structurally similar to other political parties operating in the same political system, irrespective of ideology. The sociologist Max Weber argued many years ago that there were four elements primarily involved in most party activities:

(a) Party leaders and their staffs, who are apt to play the dominant role.
(b) Active party members who for the most part merely have the function of acclamation of their leaders. Under certain circumstances, however, they may exercise some forms of control, participate in discussion, voice complaints, or even initiate revolutions within the party.
(c) The inactive masses of electors or voters, who are merely objects whose votes are sought at election time. Their attitudes are important only as an object of orientation for the soliciting of the party organization, where there are actual struggles with other parties for power.
(d) Contributors to party funds who usually, though not always, remain behind the scenes.[71]

Since Weber wrote that, we have seen the growth of the mass electorate and with it the growth of the mass party organizations, but the main contours of the major political parties have remained the same.

One essential feature of the British political system, according to many authors, is that the party organizations outside parliament are really nothing more than electioneering bodies. This is Duverger's 'modern party' with its 'functional mass membership' which has little real power

---

[71] Weber, M., in *The Theory of Social and Economic Organization*, (edited by Talcott Parsons), Oxford University Press, New York, 1947, p. 408.

within the party,[72] even through conferences. Referring to these, Lowell argued as long ago as 1908:

> ... as organs for the popular control of the party, for formulating opinion, and for ascertaining and giving effect to the wishes of the rank and file, these bodies are mere pretences ... Both are shams, but with this difference, that the Conservative organization is a transparent, and the Liberal an opaque sham.[73]

Similar sentiments have been frequently expressed about the Labour Party's participatory structure throughout its history. For instance, Shaw Desmond has written about the steady degeneration of the Labour Party into a mere 'voting machine', with the activists having little more to do than to 'get out the vote' in elections. The Labour electors, too, deserve better treatment. He quoted Tawney as saying that the Labour Party must treat electors not as voting-fodder, to be shepherded to a polling station, and then allowed to resume their slumbers, but as partners in a common enterprise, in which the Party, indeed, will play its part, but the issue of which depends ultimately on themselves'. Desmond called for 'a reversion to the original ideals of the Labour pioneers and direct opposition to the present methods and goal of organized labour.'[74] Interestingly enough, Shaw Desmond's book was published in 1921.

What then, is the nature of the Labour Party's internal organization? Is it democratic or elitist? Do the members and activists – the 'grass-roots' if you like – have any real power? What precisely is the role of Conference? The main difficulty is that it is impossible to be precise about any of these problems, and statements by Labour leaders and official party literature are exceedingly vague, contradictory, and ambiguous, especially on key questions like the role of Annual Conference. Traditionally, Labour leaders have defended Conference and have argued forcefully for the sanctity of Conference 'decisions' while on their way to the top, and have either ignored or at least have been less enthusiastic about Conference 'decisions' once they have reached the top. Attlee, for instance, wrote in *The Labour Party in Perspective* (1937)[75] about the absolute necessity of following Conference decisions and about Conference being the 'parliament of the movement', yet by the time he had become Prime Minister his enthusiasm for Conference resolutions had dramatically waned. Even Aneurin Bevan

---

[72] Duverger, M., *Political Parties: Their Organization and Activity in the Modern State*, Methuen, 1964 (3rd edn.), pp. 63–71.

[73] Lowell, A. L., *The Government of England*, London, Macmillan, 1908 (1920 edn.), vol. I, p. 584.

[74] Desmond, *op. cit.*, pp. 4 and 47.

[75] Attlee, C. R. *The Labour Party, op. cit.*

went before the Conference in the late forties to say that the PLP had no intention of abolishing 'tied cottages' despite countless Conference resolutions to that effect.

A good example neatly expressing the ambiguity surrounding the role of Conference is provided by John Parker MP's typical propagandist piece *Labour Marches On* (1947). He wrote: 'The supreme authority of the Labour Party is the Annual Party Conference . . . its instructions must be carried out by its Executive, affiliated organizations and representatives on local authorities and in Parliament . . . I have no hesitation in saying that it is a remarkably democratic institution through which a great movement thrashes out and decides Party policy.' Yet he also states that '. . . Labour leaders know that they will be in for trouble at the next Conference if they try and flout a Labour Party Conference decision'.[76] This immediately casts doubt on the veracity of the previously unambiguous statement. Nor is there much historical evidence to support Parker's contention that Conference 'instructions' must be carried out by the parliamentary representatives.

The most detailed and well-known analysis of the structure and distribution of power within the Labour Party is provided by McKenzie in his book *British Political Parties*. He asserts that the mass organization of the Labour Party outside parliament 'cannot and does not play the role so often assigned to it in partly literature'. Whether in Government or Opposition, the PLP and leadership have not been prepared to accept direction or control from Conference – 'even when the PLP has been at its weakest it has stubbornly refused to abdicate control over its own affairs'.[77] This seems pretty unequivocal stuff, but McKenzie goes on to say that in practice the channels open for mediation have ensured that the PLP is rarely out of step with the mass organization of the Party. However, McKenzie's main point is that power rests firmly with the PLP, even though party literature would seem to suggest otherwise.

The reasons why Labour leaders are so reluctant to vest control of the party in Conference are partly to do with the need to make frequent policy decisions during the parliamentary year (especially when in Opposition) in response to day-to-day events, the impracticality of running a major party on the basis of an annual four-day debate and so forth. But there are deeper reasons than that, according to McKenzie, and these are to do with the representativeness of Conference itself – something which no Labour

[76] Parker, J., *Labour Marches On*, Penguin, 1947, pp. 42–4.
[77] McKenzie, *op. cit.*, p. 455.

leader would dare to challenge, at least not in public. He quotes Beatrice Webb (in turn quoting Sidney Webb) as saying:

> Sidney observed afterwards that the Constituency Parties were frequently unrepresentative groups of nonentities dominated by fanatics and cranks, and extremists, and that if the block vote of the Trade Unions were eliminated it would be impracticable to continue to vest the control of policy in Labour Party Conferences.

McKenzie then comments:

> This statement lays bare the realities of power within the Labour Party Conference. It should be recalled that when Webb made this statement he was a member of the second Labour Government; there can be little doubt that he accurately reflected the conviction of the great majority of the Parliamentary leaders of the Labour Party then *and now*.[78]

While he is at it, McKenzie also attempts to 'de-bunk' the role of the Labour Party's regional organization and the Regional Councils. This is not too difficult, because they are constitutionally prevented even from discussing matters defined as outside their own regional area. Nevertheless, he says that the Party has been careful to ensure that the Regional Councils have very little authority, and that they exist primarily to maintain and strengthen the constituency parties, so that they may adequately perform their allotted task.

Comparing the Labour Party with the Tories, he argues that the Labour Party is the more democratic. The activities of the mass organization of the Labour Party, he says, loom larger in the affairs of the party than do similar activities of the Conservative side. The Labour Party has

> saddled itself with a party constitution which appears to vest control of party policy in the extra-parliamentary organs of the party. This has made it inevitable that the party leaders shall devote a considerable part of their time to the complex task of carrying their supporters outside Parliament with them.

But the PLP retains the initiative in the formulation and determination of policy. In no sense is the PLP the 'mouthpiece' of the 'movement', he says.

Although the mass organization of the Labour Party exerts greater in-

---

[78] *ibid.*, p. 505.

fluence than its Conservative counterpart, McKenzie argues that its primary function is the same – to work for an electoral majority for its parliamentary party. Both have a special channel of communication to the party leaderships, who cannot afford to be indifferent to the mood of the membership. However, the parliamentary leaders are not in any direct sense subject to the will of their organized supporters – 'if they were, British Parliamentary government, as presently conceived, would be unworkable.'[79] He concludes that 'the distribution of power within British political parties is primarily a function of cabinet government and the British Parliamentary system.' The two major parties are really 'two Parliamentary parties' who maintain mass organizations as 'vote-getting agencies'. Their role is to sustain 'two competing teams of Parliamentary leaders' so the electorate can choose between them.[80] But, he adds, even this limited role is diminishing as the traditional activities of the mass party – organizing public meetings, canvassing, knocking-up and so on – are of declining importance in influencing the outcome of elections. Elections are now conducted through the mass media, and the mass organizations are likely to wither away.

In fact this has still not happened. It is twenty years since McKenzie's book was first published, and the local parties have demonstrated a resilience which McKenzie had not foreseen. But there are more important problems connected with McKenzie's thesis. The first is that the McKenzie model portrays the Labour Party structure as an essentially 'closed' system. It makes it difficult to explain how change can occur in party thinking and party personnel if the existing leadership has such awful political power. But changes and policy about-turns do occur, and on many issues the party leadership has proved responsive to changes in thinking within the party and in the wider society, especially if this might mean votes. Often significant change comes about when an ambitious member of the leadership or lower ranks of the leadership detects a new mood or borrows a popular new idea or scheme, adopts it as his own, and champions it through the committees of the party hierarchy. By this mechanism, the individual's career is advanced, and the party proves itself to be responsive to change. Again, when arguments reiterated time and time again at Conference prove to be demonstrably true – like the fact that Labour was losing a lot of its young supporters to far left and community action groups in the period 1966–70, or that further road-building schemes like the

---

[79] *ibid.*, p. 558.
[80] *ibid.*, pp. 635–42.

London 'Motorway Box' did not command widespread public support – action will be initiated (perhaps belatedly and inadequately) by elements in the leadership and steps will be taken in an attempt to rectify the situation. Some might describe such actions as 'opportunist', others might say that it showed that the party was responsive to new thinking.

However, it is doubtful whether McKenzie would deny that change does occur in these and other ways. All he was saying was that the mass organization of the party has no real *power*. He did not rule out the possibility of the mass organization having *influence*. But influence is one form of power and the power of Conference, for example, is more often than not exercised in advance. Resolutions are trimmed and the National Executive Committee position is frequently modified prior to the Conference precisely in order to avoid defeats at the hands of Conference. This is not always successful, but on the important questions it usually is. Moreover, McKenzie seems to ignore the vitally important influence or power of the Trade Unions and the TUC to determine what policies will or will not be acceptable if they are placed before Conference. No NEC, for instance, would dare to put forward a proposal to Conference for a statutory incomes policy at the present time. Nor, for that matter, would the PLP dare propose one in the House.

Second, it is just not true to say that in conflicts the leadership always has its way. More often than not, when a fundamental policy dispute occurs, the leadership are forced to compromise, even if they manage to carry Conference. Sometimes they fail altogether, as the revisionists did in the debate over Clause IV in the late 50s and early 60s. But that raises a third problem.

In that protracted debate, the terms 'Revisionist' and 'Leadership' were not synonymous. The split between the revisionists and the fundamentalists occurred right up and down the party at all levels. As Beer points out, the essential error of the McKenzie model is to identify the contesting groups as 'leaders' and 'followers'. Referring to the 1951–61 period, he says that 'in fact the Party was not split, so to speak, horizontally between upper and lower echelons, but vertically between two sets of leaders and followers. At every level there was a conflict – from Shadow Cabinet through NEC and Conference to individual constituency parties and trade unions.'[81] Bevan had support in varying degrees at different levels and in different spheres of the party, as does Tony Benn today. Neither is it

---

[81] Beer, *op. cit.*, p. 231.

true to say that the CLPs are uniformly extremist and militant.

Fourth, Beer also challenges McKenzie's argument that the two major parties operate in an *essentially* similar way. His historical survey of the post-war period leads him to different conclusions. The Labour Party's 'pluralistic democracy' is 'worlds apart from the elitism of the Conservatives' and 'in practice as in theory, in the actual distribution of power as in their varying conceptions of authority, the two parties were deeply opposed'.[82]

Finally, it could be said that McKenzie's whole argument is misplaced. By comparing the distribution of power within each major party, he neglects the role of ideology and ideological differences. Admittedly, at the outset, he states that the internal distribution of power constitutes his terms of reference, which is fair enough. Yet he then goes on to argue that ideological and doctrinal factors are not relevant to our understanding of the Labour Party and that the two major parties are essentially similar in the way they operate. Moreover, despite its superficial attractions, the 'two teams' theory necessarily diminishes the role of fundamental external factors, especially the very different social bases of each party.

From the mass organization of the Labour Party we must turn our attention to the problem of the Parliamentary Labour Party itself. John Saville recently wrote:

> How it comes about that those who win elections with socialist phrases on their lips – and most are not conscious hypocrites – and then proceed to administer a capitalist society, which they have previously denounced in an as efficient way as possible, is one of the central ironies of modern British history.[83]

Within the mass organization of the Labour Party blame for Labour's frequently poor performance in office is often placed at the door of 'right wingers' in the PLP. In turn, members of the PLP and Ministers tend to blame the civil service bureaucrats for obstructing and emasculating their plans, or they blame their lack of progress on the state of the economy. A good account of the pressures and problems facing a reforming Labour minister is provided by R. H. S. Crossman in his Fabian essay 'Socialism and Planning'.[84] Immersed in the complex state structure, hampered by

---

[82] *ibid.*, p. 388 ff.

[83] Saville, J., in *Socialist Register 1967, op. cit.*, p. 53.

[84] Crossman, R. H. S., in *Socialism and Affluence: Four Fabian Essays*, Fabian Society, London, 1967.

ureaucracy, lack of information, obstruction and the parliamentary imetable, it is not surprising, he argues, that little is achieved and Labour eaders and supporters rapidly become 'worlds apart'.

Within the social sciences, the emphasis has been more on trying to xplain more fully just how and why such 'ironies' occur, why, as R. H. Tawney observed in the early thirties, 'the degeneration of socialist parties n office is now an old story'. Ever since Michels developed his 'Iron Law of Oligarchy' to explain the internal development of 'democratic' political arties, and argued that the waning radicalism of socialist parties in office vas primarily caused by the 'embourgeoisment' of its leaders, social scienists have tended to focus on party leaderships, and, in the case of the Labour Party, on the make-up of the PLP as a way of explaining why things 'go wrong'. As I pointed out above, one of the three key aspects of Parkin's 'deradicalization' argument was that the leadership of social democratic parties become the victims of bureaucratization and 'acculturation'. Michels, too, argued that socialist or social democratic party leaders were 'acculturated' into the political elite, ruling class, or establishment by accepting first, their life styles, and then their political values.

In addition, socialist leaders given the job of running the capitalist economy also face the dilemma of what Weber called the 'ethic of responsibility' versus the 'ethic of ultimate ends' – the need to keep things running in the short term, even though one might not agree with how they are run. However, 'responsibility' often presupposes acceptance of the dominant value system, and hence the only reforms which are possible are those which are 'realistic', 'realistic' being defined as being within the framework of existing values and state institutions.

Nevertheless, there is little doubt that the attitudes and views of many former Labour candidates do change once they have become MPs, the more so the longer they have been in the House. As Guttsman says:

> With few exceptions, Labour MPs submit like others to the traditions of the place, and succumb to the genus loci. Parliamentary life itself becomes an educative and moderating influence. The mores of the House lessen antagonism. The great formal egalitarianism of the rules of the House, the privileges which the Member of Parliament enjoys, and the deference shown to him by officials and servants of the House strengthen the individual's self-esteem, and do, no doubt, combat feelings of separateness. New loyalties are created . . .[85]

---

[85] Guttsman, *op. cit.*, p. 247.

The history of the Labour Party is littered with examples of radicals wh
have gone into parliament with a view to changing the world overnight an
have later modified their approach, or who, elected as socialists, end u
looking, speaking and acting like Conservatives.

How this comes about is not difficult to imagine. For instance, long ag
in 1921, Desmond quoted an editor of a 'London Conservative daily' a
saying 'some time ago' that

> Labour's opponents believe they will always be able to sidetra
> Labour, and they believe it with full justification, having regard
> Labour's record. So many of the leaders are out for themselves. An
> they lack imagination and enthusiasm. Few of them can resist a job, st
> less fewer, flattery. If they become troublesome, they can always t
> 'kicked upstairs' into office.[86]

At an earlier date, Engels had written to Lenin on the subject of th
deference displayed by many prominent Labour leaders: 'Even To
Mann, whom I regard as the best of the lot, is fond of mentioning that h
will be lunching with the Lord Mayor'.[87] Furthermore, being an MP
quite a nice life, it may be hard work, but it provides plenty of status. Man
Labour MPs have 'made it' from working class backgrounds, obscurit
and grammar schools. They themselves have benefited from th
'meritocracy', and are aware of its advantages. In order to keep their pos
tion, they must maintain the morale of their supporters – activists an
voters – and not make any silly mistakes.

They do not, of course, command mass support for a radical challenge t
the system, and to create such mass support would require too much tim
and effort. To sit back and be stifled by the cumulative weight of th
British political-cultural tradition is an easier option, just as a
acquiescence is easier than struggle. Moreover, most MPs want to be
Minister, and most Ministers want to be Prime Minister. As Finer poin
out, this factor of ambition inevitably leads the less influential to defer t
the more influential, and this too inhibits radical departures from existin
tradition.[88] Finally, to the Labour MP, the easy-going virtues of bourgeo
democracy are infinitely preferable to what most see as the main (an
abhorrent) alternative of totalitarianism, either Soviet or Fascist.

The manner in which the character of Labour's leadership cadre has u
dergone change has also been portrayed by Guttsman. He argues that i

---

[86] Desmond, op. cit., p. 75.
[87] Lenin, V. I., in 'Lenin On Britain', op. cit., p. 144.
[88] Finer, S. E., Comparative Government, Pelican, 1974, p. 173.

the early days Labour's leaders came mainly from three groups: officials of sympathizing trade unions who were active in municipal politics and in the House of Commons, a small group of socialist propagandists, publicists and intellectuals, and a number of prominent local leaders who set out to organize socialist supporters in the industrial areas. But, he says, the political leadership of the Labour Party has now become institutionalized:

> Parliamentary activity or Trade Union leadership has now become *the* road to political eminence. Today, political reputation is increasingly made in Parliament itself or in junior office, and selection occurs largely through the existing leadership. It is only when a vociferous and able opposition group in the PLP succeeds in gaining first the ear and then the votes of an active minority in local party organizations, as was the case with the Bevanite rebels, that a change in the composition of the Party leadership can take place.[89]

What then, have been suggested as the overall functions of the Labour Party? We have looked at some aspects of the structure of the Labour Party, and have attempted to demonstrate how the structure of the Party has been tailored to suit the original and manifest function of the Labour Party – participating in elections with a view to getting Labour candidates elected to parliament. But some have argued that it is possible to make other, higher-level generalizations which bring into focus the more hidden or latent functions of the Labour Party. Three lines of argument are worthy of note.

The first is that the smooth operation of capitalist democracy requires different interest groups to be 'represented' in some way by organizations purportedly 'representing' them. If a major section of society like the working class went completely unrecognized and unrepresented, then this would amount to a structural weakness in the system – storing up trouble for the future, if you like. Therefore, for the sake of social stability, it is generally agreed that the TUC's job, for instance, is to represent the workers, and the CBI's is to represent businessmen, and each political party represents a different section of society. As Seymour Lipset, the father of the theory of 'pluralist democracy', argued: 'a stable democracy requires consensus on the nature of the political struggle, and this includes the assumption that different groups are best served by different parties.'[90]

---

[89] Guttsman, *op. cit.*, pp. 272–3.

[90] Lipset, S. M., *Political Man*, Heinemann, 1960, p. 408.

The *representation* of interests through political parties is therefore 'func tional' to maintenance of capitalist democracy.

The second is that if classes are one of the key structural features o capitalist society, then the channelling of class interests through *participa tion* in the political system is also 'functional' to that system. According t Kornhauser's theory of 'mass society', if substantial sections of the popula tion are not given any opportunity to participate in the political systen through political parties, pressure groups and voluntary organizations then this is not conducive to social integration and the maintenance o capitalist democracy.[91] An unstable, alienated 'mass' society develops, breeding ground for totalitarian movements. From this perspective, it i clear that the main problem in recent times in Britain has been the integra tion of the working class into the political system, since the middle clas have always participated in above average proportions, i.e. they have bee well integrated. The Labour Party is seen as the main avenue of workin class participation, and hence the main integrative mechanism. Workin class participation through the Labour Party is therefore 'functional' to th maintenance of capitalist democracy.

Third, Miliband (and others) have extended this argument to the Labou Party itself, putting forward a kind of 'containment' theory. Actually hi argument is not a lot different from the two above, but it is based more o an analysis of the history of the Labour Party, rather than political o sociological theory. The Labour Party, he says, has acted as 'safety valve for the British ruling class who have seen it as the best antidote to rea socialism and revolution.[92] The capitalist system actually requires such party because it plays a crucial role in the 'management of discontent'. I keeps class feeling and protest within safe bounds.[93] By making onl moderate and reformist demands, the Labour movement itself has prove highly 'functional' to the maintenance of capitalist society, and has allowe the ruling class to demonstrate that it is not incapable of meeting th limited demands of Labour.[94] However, he concludes that there is no much reason to think that the ruling class cannot continue to gran concessions.

But Miliband was writing over ten years ago, and the ability to gran concessions under pressure from Labour is largely dependent on economi

---

[91] See Berry, D., *The Sociology of Grass Roots Politics*, Macmillan, 1970.

[92] Miliband, *Parliamentary Socialism*, *op. cit.*, p. 37.

[93] *ibid.*, p. 376.

[94] Miliband, in *Socialist Register 1964*, Merlin Press, 1964, p. 95 and pp. 101–2, and in *Sociali Register 1966*, p. 24.

growth – the continued increase in production, productivity and the 'size of the cake'. In a situation of nil economic growth, the ability to satisfy even moderate demands is severely curtailed. As Bonham pointed out some years ago (in a statement which provides, incidentally, an interesting slant on the argument of some contemporary Labour Party leaders that we cannot have income redistribution without economic growth):

> The need for higher productivity is often presented as an economic question, but to the middle class it is also the political heart of the matter. Can the nation produce enough real wealth to satisfy the working class majority, and so avoid another attack on the living standards of those above the average?[95]

There is one further refinement of the argument that working class representation and participation is 'good' for capitalism and that is the 'institutionalization of social conflict'. By accepting political conflict and industrial conflict, and by institutionalizing it by means of the political parties on the one hand and the trade unions and employer's organizations on the other, each type of conflict is isolated from other types, and fundamental class conflict is fragmented into separate 'industrial' and 'political' disputes. In this sense, says Mann, the Labour Party and the trade unions are essentially *capitalist* organizations since the fragmentation of social conflict is one of the key characteristics of all capitalist societies.

The main problem with this perspective, as with all 'functionalist' theories, is that it provides an easy way of 'explaining' something without really explaining much at all. Faced with the problem of explaining the existence of the Labour Party, the functionalist replies by saying that it exists because it is 'functional' to the maintenance of the system. Now I don't want for one moment to deny the value of this line of argument in helping us understand certain aspects of the Labour Party, but it might equally be possible to make out a case that the *non*-existence of the Labour Party – and, say, the imposition of a fascist dictatorship – would be more 'functional' for capitalism.

A Working Class Party?

A number of surveys have found that the majority of Labour Party supporters, especially working class members, see the Labour Party over-

---

[95] Bonham, J., *The Middle Class Vote*, Faber and Faber, 1954, p. 196.

whelmingly as 'the party of the working class'. As we shall see below, at the local level this is probably still the case, the Hindess' 'middle class take-over' has not yet materialized. But at the national level, the Labour Party does indeed appear to be less of a working class party than at any time in its history.

I say 'appears to be', first because the argument that the Labour Party is becoming dominated by 'middle class' elements is usually based on statistics for the occupational background of Labour MPs, and these must be treated with some caution. Second, it is evident from history that the Labour Party has always had a disproportionate percentage of middle class people in its parliamentary leadership, disproportionate that is, in relation to the class make-up of the Labour electorate. Let us look at some facts.

Guttsman says that in 1906, the twenty-nine men who were elected un-der LRC auspices, were, without exception, of working class background. But from then on the percentage of Labour MPs who had originally followed indubitably working class occupations fell from 100 per cent to 92 per cent in 1918, 70 per cent in 1924, 60 per cent in 1929, rising slightly to 64 per cent in 1935.[96] By far the largest percentage increase was recorded in the 'professional' category. After the war, the process continued so that by 1970 the proportions of 'professionals' and 'workers' had all but been reversed. According to the Nuffield election studies, the percentage of Labour MPs who had previously followed professional occupations in-creased from 49 per cent in 1955 to 61 per cent in 1970. The proportion of all 'workers', manual and white collar, had dropped from 42 per cent to 31 per cent over the same period, while the strictly 'manual' category fell from 35 per cent to 25 per cent of the PLP. As Johnson points out, the proportion of the PLP in the 1970 parliament drawn from the professions was actually higher than the Tory proportion, although it is interesting to note that most of the Labour professionals were teachers, lecturers and lawyers, whereas most of the Tory professionals were company directors, doctors and lawyers.[97] Moreover, he argues that this trend is bound to continue, judging by the pattern of recent recruitment, the age of the ex-manual working class MPs and the party's B list of potential candidates.

But many of today's Labour MPs are really second generation working class often tied to the Labour movement by strong emotional and family links. For instance, in 1973 there were twenty ex-miners sitting as MPs, but forty sons of miners. Much of the decline can also be explained by the

---

[96] Guttsman, *op. cit.*, p. 237.
[97] Johnson, R. W., 'The Political Elite', *New Society*, 24 Jan., 1974.

ack of interest now shown by the Trade Unions in the House of Commons tself and in insisting upon the sponsorship of working class candidates. Most important of all, wider educational opportunities have meant that a far higher proportion of articulate working class children have entered middle class occupations through the medium of higher education. As George Brown recently suggested, 'An Ernie Bevin born today would almost certainly go to university and become an economist, statistician, or businessman'.[98] He is less likely to become a local Labour leader or to work his way up the Trade Union ladder from the bottom rung.

Two other reasons may be forwarded to explain the 'rise of the middle class' within the PLP. The first is that it is part of an overall professionalization' of politics in Britain in the twentieth century. Guttsman, for instance, argues that a comparatively new development has been the 'professional politician', made necessary by the complexity of modern government. He writes:

The development of the Labour leadership ... highlights the changing character of a cadre of politicians in a highly complex democratic society. It illustrates quite clearly the trend away from politicians who live *for* politics to those who live *by* politics. The number of politicians for whom politics is not only a way of life but a livelihood has been steadily increasing in our society.[99]

The second reason is linked to this. With the growing sophistication of politics, working class participants have found themselves to be even more disadvantaged than they already were, and this is true at all levels including the parliamentary. Often outmanoeuvred by the more articulate and verbally skilled middle class politician, the working class politician is less likely to be able to manifest the kind of 'ability' which is looked for in the parliamentary situation. Moreover, it has even been suggested that the lack of a university training in ideas and analysis is a further handicap. Nevertheless, it is clear that working class people are severely handicapped in any number of ways when they come to participate in the political system. It led Wilkinson to conclude that 'in modern British history, this role of the middle classes in building up and dominating the mass parties has been a seriously neglected theme, especially in regard to the Labour Party'.[100]

---

[98] Brown, G., *In My Way*, Gollancz, 1971, p. 84.
[99] Guttsmann, *op. cit.*, p. 245.
[100] Wilkinson, P., *Social Movement*, Macmillan, 1971, p. 133.

The bias against working class participation in our political system wa evident in the Labour Party very early on. I have already outlined, for instance, the role of the middle class Fabians who exerted, for better or for worse, an influence out of all proportion to their numbers. And Williams reference in his description of the LRC Founding Conference to the 'groups of working class men, interspersed here and there with a few of a more professional kind . . .'[101] might have ignored the fact that it was the few who were pulling the strings. Moreover, some of the early Labour leaders like Ramsay MacDonald went out of their way to attract middle class recruits in order to give Labour a more 'respectable' image.[102] In the 1920s, there was an influx of not just middle class, but aristocratic recruits into the Labour Party, attracted partly by principle, and partly by the possibility of high office. Although Cline, in her study of the aristocratic 'Recruits to Labour'[103] concludes that their influence was not very great, other writers at the time, like Egon Wertheimer, argued forcefully that they were contributing to the dilution of Labour Party ideology.[104] It was, he argued, far too easy for the middle class to join the Labour Party, since membership required no real socialist commitment.

Throughout this general review of Labourism, I have attempted to focus on certain aspects of the Labour Party which are relevant to an appraisal of the various 'de-radicalization' theses. This required, among other things, a clarification of the origins and character of Labourism, an examination of the relationship between the Labour Party and socialism, and an outline of how the Labour Party works. In the following chapter, we will be taking a look at local Labour parties, because an understanding of the operation of local Labour parties greatly assists our understanding of the Labour Party as a whole.

We will begin by outlining just what is known about local Labour parties, gleaned from surveys, studies and various observations which have been made over the years. We will then be in a position, first, to examine Hindess' four conclusions about changes allegedly occurring in the local Labour parties (see page 28 above) in relation to other arguments and survey evidence. And second, drawing on historical material, it will be possible to say something about the role of the Labour Party in the local community, and to draw some appropriate conclusions.

[101] Williams, F., *op. cit.*, p. 10.
[102] Barker, *op. cit.*, p. 102.
[103] Cline, C. A., *Recruits to Labour: the British Labour Party 1914–31*, Syracuse, New York, 1963.
[104] Wertheimer, *op. cit.*, p. 89 and pp. 114–17.

4. Labour in the Local Community

Constituency Labour Parties:
Turnout, Membership and Participation

Without denying for one moment the value of more general historical and sociological accounts of the Labour Party, I hope to make it clear in this chapter that there is a sense in which Labour's problems begin and end in the grass roots, a sense in which the achievements and failings of Labourism at the national level are mirrored at the local level, a sense in which constituency Labour parties are a microcosm of the national Labour Party.

Very little is known about local Labour parties, and more especially, about the flavour of local Labour politics in different historical periods. For instance, in the second volume of Alan Beattie's survey of English party politics, it is interesting to note that the two sections on 'the party in the country' are by far the thinnest in terms of documentary sources, compared with the chapters on 'party rhetoric' and 'the party in Parliament'; and Beattie himself points up the problem of finding out what was really happening in party politics at the local level.[1]

As early as 1900, the LRC set up a committee to report on the best form of constituency organization, and in 1901 it was recommended (and accepted) that no uniform system be started yet, but that local organization would be left for the time being to affiliated bodies, mainly the existing socialist societies.[2] But some local LRCs did emerge out of joint meetings between local trades councils, trade unions and socialist societies. In fact, there were about a hundred local, but small, LRCs in existence by 1906.

---

[1] Beattie, A. (ed.), *English Party Politics*, vol II, *The Twentieth Century*, Weidenfeld and Nicolson, 1970, p. 237.

[2] See McKenzie, *British Political Parties*, Heinemann, 1963 (2nd edn.), pp. 467 ff.

One or two like Woolwich and Barnard Castle instituted individual membership, and these were the forerunners of today's CLPs. The accepted wisdom is that for many years, and certainly until 1918, it was one of the socialist societies, the Independent Labour Party, which provided the essential framework and the great bulk of branches of Labour's constituency organization. It is pointed out that the ILP had 672 branches in 1918, and the LRC only 158. Yet most of the former were tiny, and only 244 were represented at the 1914 Annual Conference. Williams says that 'it was only through the ILP that the working man or woman could join the Labour Party and work for it. The ILP provided most of the speakers in the country, it did most of the campaigning and practically all the propaganda'. Indeed, he says that 'over most of the country, the ILP was the Labour Party.'[3] But the Trade Unions controlled the block votes of the Annual Conference, and most matters, including sometimes even the selection of candidates, were decided at the national level, so this divorce of functions was bound to lead to tensions, tensions which are still present in the Labour Party today.

However, it has also been argued recently that the ILP was not as important as most have made out, especially after 1910, and even more so after 1918. R. I. McKibbin argues that it was the Trade Unions who were responsible for the growth of the Labour Party at the local level after 1910, and they 'bore the weight' of local organization after 1918. The ILP found it impossible to match the efforts of the Trade Unions, especially in terms of finance.[4] Although Constituency Labour Parties proper were instituted at the 1918 Conference, little growth was experienced until 1924, when, under the direction of Arthur Henderson, the number of CLPs rapidly increased. But the whole country was not covered until around 1932, thirty two years after the formation of the LRC.

According to Transport House's model rules, Constituency Labour Parties are 'the operative units of party activity' and the primary purpose of each ward association within each constituency party is defined as 'maintaining the necessary machinery for elections within its area, and, with the approval of the executive committee of the (Constituency) Party, undertaking propaganda work'.[5] An official publication, *Party Organisation*, by H. Croft (1950), talks of wards being subdivided into polling district sub-

---

[3] Williams, F., *Fifty Years March – the Rise of the Labour Party*, Odhams, 1950, p. 203.

[4] McKibbin, R. I., 'The Evolution of a National Party: Labour's Political Organisation 1910–24, D.Phil. dissertation (Oxford), 1970. Now published as *The Evolution of the Labour Party 1910–24*, Oxford, 1975.

[5] McKenzie, *op. cit.*, pp. 538–45.

committees and the use of 'street captains' – party organizers in every street. And a similar semi-official book on *The Labour Party Today* (1939), by Mary Agnes Hamilton says that

> The local Parties are the living and growing units of the steadily advancing strength of Labour in the nation. They are the great training schools of service. ... In them, day by day, there is given that devoted, unpaid, freely-rendered work by great numbers of men and women, often unheard of outside their own area.[6]

It is most likely that these accounts are expressing what *should* be the case, an ideal rather than the reality. McKenzie concludes from his studies that Croft's account of ward organization 'would appear to be a somewhat idealized conception of how ward sub-committees should function'.[7] A succession of articles by various authors throughout the 1950s and 60s in the *Fabian Journal, Socialist Commentary,* the *New Statesman, Tribune* and other influential publications, drew attention to the parlous state of Labour's local organizations.[8] The response from Transport House was to initiate two special inquiries, resulting in the Wilson Report of 1955, and the Simpson Report of 1968, both of which made certain recommendations for improving the 'penny farthing machine'. Few would seriously argue that these actually achieved anything.

What, then, *is* the reality of Labour's local organizations? And has there been 'an absolute decline in voting and in other forms of orthodox political activity' connected with the Labour Party, as Hindess suggests? In order to examine this statement, and to throw some light on the workings of local Labour parties over the years, we need to look at first, the evidence concerning electoral turnout, second, local Labour party membership levels and trends, and third, the extent and nature of participation in orthodox Labour activity.

For General Elections, Butler and Stokes tell us that

> the weakening of Labour's identification with distinctively working class goals is also consistent with the notable fall of electoral turnout in traditional working class strongholds. Indeed, a lessening of the perceived difference between the parties in class terms may have a great

---

[6] Hamilton, M. A., *The Labour Party Today,* Labour Book Service, 1939, pp. 62–3. See also Parker, J., *Labour Marches On,* Penguin, 1947, p. 50.

[7] McKenzie, *op. cit.,* p. 546.

[8] For the debate on Labour's organization, see references in the selected bibliography, pp. 158–162.

deal to do with the general fall in turnout in the country, down from 84 per cent in 1950, to 75 per cent in 1966.[9]

This misleading statement neatly ignores the lowish 72·8 per cent turnout in the Labour landslide of 1945, and the still lower turnouts registered between the wars. The UK figures for turnout since 1918 vary considerably, but they demonstrate clearly the extraordinary peak in electoral activity in 1950–51, and the subsequent steady decline down to June 1970. But even before then, it would have been entirely inappropriate to suggest a long term decline in voting. Quite the contrary. At an average of 79·1 per cent for the fifties and sixties, turnout was still a clear 5 per cent above the 74·1 per cent average for the twenties and thirties.

Percentage Turnout in General Elections since 1918 (UK average)[10]

1918: 57·2	1935: 71·1	1964: 77·1
1922: 73·0	1945: 72·8	1966: 75·8
1923: 71·1	1950: 83·9	1970: 72·0
1924: 77·0	1951: 82·6	1974: 79·0
1929: 76·3	1955: 76·8	1974: 72·8
1931: 76·4	1959: 78·7	

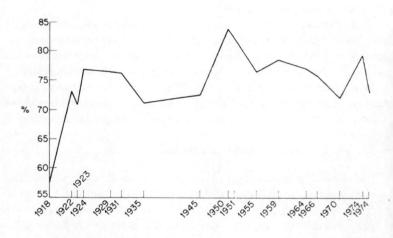

---

[9] Butler, D., and Stokes, D., *Political Change in Britain: Forces Shaping Electoral Choice*, Pelican, 1971, pp. 155–6.

[10] Craig, F. W. S., *British Parliamentary Election Statistics 1918–70*, Political Reference Publications, 1970, pp. 46–7.

As evidence for their argument that the decline in turnout was associated with a 'lessening of the perceived difference between the parties in class terms' Butler and Stokes cite the fall in turnout in 'solid working class areas, especially the mining seats' — down by $3 \cdot 8$ per cent in mining areas and $3 \cdot 6$ per cent in large cities between 1955 and 1966. But once again, the selection of these dates has no special significance, the changes are not great, there may be other reasons for the decline — especially in large cities where the population is becoming more and more mobile — and in any case, the 'trend' has now been reversed. Moreover, if the slight decline registered in this period was related to a 'lessening of the perceived difference between the parties in class terms', how do we explain the lower turnouts before? Did people perceive that the parties differed less in class terms in 1945? or 1935? or in 1923?

For local municipal elections, the Registrar General has published annually since 1946 turnout figures for all local elections in England and Wales, including the average turnout for elections to the four different types of local authority — Counties, County Boroughs, Urban Districts/Municipal Boroughs and Rural Districts. The overall (unweighted) average since 1946 shows that a poll of 50 per cent or more has only been achieved in one post-war year, 1947, and a similar turnout in any type of local election has only been achieved in three years — 1947, 1948 and 1952. A steady decline since 1947 has been broken only by peaks of 48 per cent and 44 per cent in 1952 and 1963. From an average turnout of $48 \cdot 0$ per cent in the period 1947–52, turnout has fallen significantly to $38 \cdot 5$ per cent in 1966–71. A slight rise to around 40 per cent in 1971 was caused merely by the fact that there were no County Council elections in that year, and these elections generally experience abysmally low turnouts, presumably due to the remoteness and size of each authority. In fact more detailed figures presented in the Registrar General's 1967 Review and earlier studies by Rhodes, Birch, and Political and Economic Planning, show a clear correlation between the size of an authority and participation in it.[11] But the decline in turnout since 1947 has been most marked in County Boroughs and in Rural Districts, where we would expect there to have been a greater decline in 'community' over the last two and a half

---

[11] See Rhodes, E. C., 'Voting at Municipal Elections', *Political Quarterly*, 1938, vol. 9, no. 2, pp. 271–80; *idem.*, 'The Exercise of the Franchise in London', *Political Quarterly*, 1938, vol. 9, no. 1, pp. 113–19; Birch, A. H., 'The Habit of Voting', *Manchester School*, 1950, vol. 18, no. 1, pp. 75–82; Political and Economic Planning, 'Active Democracy — A Local Election', *Planning*, 1947, vol. 13, no. 261, pp. 1–20; *idem.*, 'Local Elections — How Many Vote?', *Planning*, 1948, vol. 13, no. 291, pp. 163–78.

decades. Where slightly more intimate social relationships prevail in the small Urban Districts and Municipal Boroughs, the decline has been less marked.

Percentage Turnout in Municipal Elections Since 1946
(UK Average)[12]

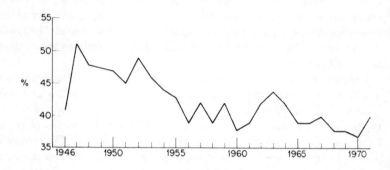

There is no doubt that the immediate post-war period saw an upsurge in political participation of all kinds, though voting in formal elections is only one dimension of this. A 1948 Political and Economic Planning pamphlet was able to state that

> the success of the democratic system in war has given it a new prestige and has made us more conscious of its values. . . . There has been an increase of interest and of participation in the British system of government at both ends of the scale. . . . even the humblest of local elections – for Parish Councils – have aroused an interest which is unprecedented.[13]

Yet the indications are that the subsequent decline has gone further than a mere return to pre-war levels of participation (when the local franchise was more restricted).

A survey of 77 'major cities' carried out by E. C. Rhodes in 1938 revealed that turnout in local elections between 1921 and 1928 averaged 52 per cent. Between 1930 and 1937 the average was 48 per cent, ranging from 34 per cent in the case of Birmingham to 73 per cent in Barnsley. Both these

---

[12] The Registrar General's *Annual Statistical Review of England and Wales*, HMSO, 1946–71.
[13] P.E.P., 'Active Democracy – A Local Election', *op. cit.*, p. 1.

figures are well above the 43 per cent achieved in the 1960s.[14] On the other hand, a survey of turnout between 1933 and 1938 in a smaller sample of County Boroughs, Counties, Non-County Boroughs, Urban Districts and Rural Districts indicated that the median turnout in the County Boroughs was under 40 per cent. For the other kinds of local authority it was even lower – less than 20 per cent for County Council elections, and less than 10 per cent for Rural District elections.[15]

So the national evidence on turnout is mixed, and in particular the lack of easily available figures for electoral turnout in traditional Labour areas over the last half-century (which would be specially relevant to Hindess' argument) prevents firm conclusions being drawn. Moreover, as Sharpe points out in his study of London County Council elections, although the percentage of the *electorate* voting had declined from around 50 per cent at the turn of the century to an average of 31·5 per cent between 1945 and 1960 (with the lowest polls occurring in the 1920s and 1930s), the percentage of the *population* voting had increased along with the widening of the franchise. For instance, only 12 per cent of the population had the vote in 1899, compared with 69 per cent in 1961, and one man one vote was only introduced in local government in 1948. There is therefore a long term trend upwards in the percentage of the population voting, but the percentage of the electorate voting is apparently going down.[16]

Another traditional area for which we do have a complete run of figures for turnout in municipal elections is the City of Sheffield. In his study of politics in Sheffield, Hampton provides turnout statistics for every election between 1918 and 1969.[17] These, too, show a steady decline, but Hampton also suggests a plausible reason why this should be so, a reason not necessarily connected with the overall theme of the Hindess argument – that there has been a progressive working class disillusionment with the Labour Party and bourgeois democracy. Turnout in Sheffield has declined quite dramatically from an average of 50·4 per cent in the 1920s and 49·2 per cent in the 1930s to 47·3 per cent in the late 1940s, 34·0 per cent in the 1950s and a mere 29·7 per cent during the 1960s. But this may only be an extreme example of the effect of marginality on turnout and may be indicative of a greater sophistication on the part of the electorate. It would suggest that turnout is low in Sheffield because the vast majority of wards

---

[14] Rhodes, 'Voting at Municipal Elections', *op. cit.*

[15] 'Turnout in Local Elections', *Fabian Quarterly*, no. 46 (1945).

[16] Sharpe, L. J., *A Metropolis Votes*, LSE, 1962, pp. 22–4.

[17] Hampton, W., *Democracy and Community: A Study of Politics in Sheffield*, Oxford University Press, 1970, p. 313.

are safely Labour-held (as is the City Council), and a significant proportion of individual electors may well feel that they need not bother to vote as the result is a foregone conclusion. This is borne out by a detailed breakdown of the figures which shows that turnout in marginal wards since 1945 has averaged 43 per cent, while turnout in the safe Labour wards has averaged 29 per cent. It is also borne out by Hampton's interviews with electors, whose replies suggest that 'the effectiveness of an individual vote *is* consciously considered by many voters'.[18] Labour voters in particular have traditionally been more 'instrumental' in their approach to voting – they are more likely only to turnout and vote if there is a chance that their vote will actually make any difference – whereas it has been generally accepted that Tory voters are more 'expressive' – they are more likely to use their vote anyway, irrespective of whether it will achieve anything. Previous studies in the field of electoral turnout have also indicated that turnout rates can be correlated with other 'non-ideological' factors such as the housing density of a particular area, the rate of population turnover, and the actual size of a particular town or city (see footnote 11 above). Even the physical structure of an area affects political participation rates. For instance, turnout from multi-occupied houses and tower blocks is generally lower than that from terraced or semi-detached houses occupied by single families. With the increasing population turnover in some areas of our cities, the break-up of many traditional working class communities, the demolition of large areas of terraced housing, and the transfer of the occupants to outlying estates or multi-storey tower blocks, it might be expected that there would be pressure for political participation rates to fall for the country as a whole. As we shall see in the next chapter, in areas such as Brighton where most of the social fabric has remained essentially the same for many decades, electoral turnout rates have also remained much the same.

Returning now to local Labour parties as such, membership levels are one area where we would expect to see some decline if the first proposition of the 'decline of working class politics' thesis is broadly correct. Once again, definitive conclusions are somewhat problematical because the evidence on membership of Constituency Labour Parties, past and present, needs to be interpreted carefully. First, the membership lists kept by each constituency party are notoriously unreliable, and it is often difficult to say just who is and who is not a party 'member'. Second, since the 1st January 1963 the minimum figure upon which CLPs can affiliate to the Party has

---

[18] *ibid.*, p. 169.

been 1000. Most CLPs claim 1000 members but in reality their membership is a lot less.

Individual Membership of the Labour Party 1928–1972
(Official Figures)

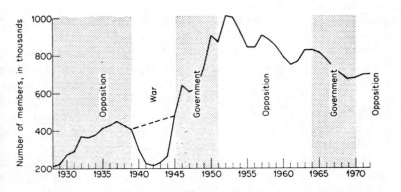

According to official figures, the individual membership of the Labour Party currently stands at just over 700,000 or around 6 per cent of the Labour electorate – and by far the lowest ratio of members to electors of the European social democratic parties. As the graph shows, after peaking at 1,015,000 in 1952, official membership had fallen to just over 700,000 by 1972, declining most rapidly between 1953 and 1955, 1957 and 1961, and between 1965 and 1969. From these figures it would not therefore seem to be the case that the decline during the 1966–70 Labour government was the most catastrophic in the history of the party. But, it should be noted, the official figures obscure the 'cushioning' effect of the 1000 minimum affiliation rule, which did not apply in other earlier periods. Any decline in any CLP *below* 1000 goes unrecorded in the official total, as does any increase below 1000. Therefore, the small overall increase registered in 1971 and 1972 – a period when it is known that many CLPs were recruiting new members in large numbers – some even doubling or trebling their membership – gives some idea of the extent of the decline between 1965 and 1970. In 1969, only 111 CLPs claimed over 1000 members (down from 225 in 1966), but Butler and Pinto-Duschinsky suggest that 80 would be a

more accurate figure.[19] They cite the results of an NEC Inquiry into the 1.
Glasgow CLPs in 1969 (which revealed that there were only 1786 Labour
Party members in the whole of Glasgow – some CLPs had less than 50
members) in support of their contention that most CLPs have between 350
and 500 members. Together with those that claim over 1000 members (and
an average of 1170) this gives an approximate average total membership of
the Labour Party for the period 1964 to 1970 of between 310,000 and
385,000, not nearly 700,000 as was claimed. This represents only around :
per cent of the Labour electorate.

Dean carried out a similar check in Birmingham in late 1970, and found
that the average membership of 13 Birmingham CLPs was only 390. He es-
timates that 'the true membership of the Labour Party could be as low as
one-third of the official figures and almost certainly no more than one-half
of the official total'.[20] City parties seem to do particularly badly, only 7 out
of 98 provincial city CLPs even *claimed* over 1000 members in 1969, and
both Leeds and Liverpool had no full-time agents at all. In addition, only
23 per cent of the CLPs in safe Labour seats claimed memberships of over
1000, while 54 per cent did so in seats marginally-held by Labour.

However, while the Labour Party lost one-third of its individual
members – and probably more than half – between 1951 and 1972, the
Tories faced similar problems. National membership of the Conservative
Party fell from 2·8 million in 1953 to less than 1·4 million in 1969–70 – a
greater absolute loss, but proportionately about the same. This would seem
to suggest that any explanation of this trend of declining membership cannot be specific to the Labour Party. The decline in Labour Party
membership is more likely to be part of a general process affecting all
political parties and maybe all voluntary organizations, perhaps a trend
toward the increasing 'privatization' of life-styles. There has been no
'decline of working class politics' in the Hindess sense for those who have
left the Conservative Party. Yet, ironically, because the Conservative Party
has many more individual members than the Labour Party, and given the
more broadly-based nature of Conservative electoral support, it is quite
probable that the Conservatives actually have more working class
members than the Labour Party!

As to the earlier trends in Labour Party membership, two points could
be made. The first is that, contrary to popular belief, Labour Party

[19] Butler, D., and Pinto-Duschinsky, M., *The British General Election of 1970*, Macmillan, 1971, pp.
264–78.

[20] Dean, M., 'Is Labour Dying?', *Guardian*, 18–21 Jan. 1971. See also Paul Foot, *Sunday Times*,
29 Sept. 1968.

membership remained comparatively low throughout the 1920s and 1930s. For most of the period, it continued to climb steadily, although it actually began to decline again after 1937. The second is that, along with the unprecedented upsurge in political activity after the Second World War, Labour Party membership rapidly climbed to an all-time peak. A short period of perhaps half a dozen years in the late 1940s and early 1950s was very much the heyday of constituency labour parties, and this has been affirmed by a number of local studies.

For instance, according to Benney *et al.*, Greenwich CLP had no less than 3,800 members in 1949, a figure never since equalled.[21] Gould's study of Riverside CLP revealed over 2000 members between 1951 and 1953, compared with only 275 in 1930 and 200 in 1939.[22] Even more significant, Bealey *et al*,'s detailed study of the evolution of the Labour Party in the mining and pottery constituency of Newcastle-under-Lyme showed how the total membership of the CLP rose from 700 in 1947, to 1000 in 1948, and to 2000 in 1949. They found that some wards reported ten or fifteenfold increases on the pre-war figures, but, subsequent to 1952–3, a gradual but steady decline set in. Total membership was down to 426 by 1959–60.[23]

A similar picture emerges when we look at participation levels in local Labour parties. Once again, the evidence is sporadic and fragmentary, but from the few studies that have been undertaken we do know enough to be able to draw some conclusions about the extent to which Labour members and electors engage in orthodox political activity through their local Labour Parties. It is also possible to indicate which recent historical periods have seen either a growth or decline of participation in orthodox Labour Party activity, and to say something about the nature of that activity. This is all the more easy in that most surveys have produced very similar conclusions.

Local Labour parties have always been characterized by low levels of activity and participation among their membership. Only a small percentage of members are, and have been, remotely active in their local party. Gould, for instance, in his study of 'Riverside' CLP conducted during the 'heyday' of CLPs in the early 1950s, found that the 'active politicals' in the constituency did not number more than 100 members out of a total

[21] Benney, M., Gray, A. P. and Pear, R. H., *How People Vote: A study of Electoral Behaviour in Greenwich*, Routledge, 1956.

[22] Gould, J., 'Riverside', *Fabian Journal*, 1954, no. 14, p. 48.

[23] Bealey, F., Blondel, J., McCann, W. P., *Constituency Politics: A study of Newcastle-under-Lyme*, Faber, 1965.

membership of over 2000 and 'for many of them activity does not amount to more than attendance at periodical ward meetings'. Moreover, though the total membership was still moving upwards at the time, Gould found that the net gain of actual activists was minimal. He found that ward meetings were seldom attended by more than a 'fraction' of the paper membership, which led him to conclude that wards were being merely kept 'ticking over' until the next election.[24] Similarly, Donnison and Plowman, in their study of the Manchester (Gorton) party, found that only 11 per cent of the membership claimed to have attended a ward meeting in the last month, and only 19 per cent claimed that they had in the previous six months.[25]

Their level of 'political knowledge' was 'not high'. Again this survey was carried out in the heyday of the early 1950s. As to the character of Labour Party meetings, they also carried out a minute-by-minute survey of seven management committee meetings in Stretford Labour Party, which revealed that no less than 74 per cent of the proceedings was spent discussing administrative matters and only 20 per cent of the time was spent discussing policy.

A Fabian study of 36 wards in Manchester which included a questionnaire survey of 800 members and a content analysis of nine ward meetings emphasized the same point.[26] The cumbersomely democratic procedure, they write, 'make for dull meetings and sparse attendance; indeed, it is only by keeping their meetings small that some wards are able to curtail discussion of business sufficiently to get anything done at all'.[27] There are other reasons, too, if a recent statement by Labour Party General Secretary Ron Hayward is anything to go by: 'Some Parties don't want new members. They have got a nice little comfortable clique and don't want new faces to upset them.'[28]

The Fabian researchers found an average of only 18 attending ward meetings in Manchester in this 'heyday' period, and their description conveys something of the flavour of local Labour Parties at this time:

Labour's local organization is built on its ward parties, which hold meetings each month, generally in a school, a community centre or a

[24] Gould, *op. cit.*, p. 14.

[25] Donnison, D. V., and Plowman, D. E. G., 'The Functions of Local Labour Parties', *Political Studies*, 1954, vol. 2, pp. 154–67.

[26] Wilfred Fienburgh MP and the Manchester Fabian Society, 'Put Policy On The Agenda', *Fabian Journal*, Feb. 1952, no. 6.

[27] *ibid.*, p. 28.

[28] *Labour Weekly*, 14.4.72.

church hall. Most wards have many other activities too: summer out-
ings, a Labour League of Youth, a Women's Group, and social evenings,
perhaps twice a week, with music, dancing and refreshments. Labour
Party pamphlets are often on sale at meetings and many wards print a
news-sheet which is distributed to members each month when their
subscriptions are collected. It will be seen from this list that many of the
ward parties' activities are 'social' rather than political, and monthly
meetings often have a similar character.[29]

Milne and MacKenzie, in their book *Marginal Seat 1955* — an account of
the 1955 General Election in Bristol North-East — say that they found
Labour Party meetings exactly as described in the Fabian survey. They
also point out that attendance at Labour Party public meetings was very
low in this period, averaging only 30 throughout the campaign.[30] Neither
were the Fabians alone in suggesting that local Labour Party activities
like all political party and voluntary association activities, are essentially
'social' in character. Birch, in his study of 'small town politics', concluded
that the local political parties were 'social' rather than 'political'
organizations.[31]

Berry, in *The Sociology of Grass Roots Politics*, a study of political participation in Liverpool, Walton, asked his sample of Labour Party
members how and why they came to join the Labour Party, and only 30 per
cent mentioned party politics or political principles. Twenty-one per cent
said that they joined because of the attraction of the Labour Social Club,
and 46 per cent replied in terms of the influence of family ties, relatives,
husbands and wives.[32]

One of the best accounts of the evolution of a local Labour party over a
number of years is provided in Bealey, Blondel and McCann's study of constituency politics in Newcastle-under-Lyme, mentioned above. They
detail how the Newcastle Labour Party was almost non-existent in the
1930s. Local miners showed little interest, it achieved very few electoral
successes, and even ceased to function in 1937. The 1939–45 War, of
course, changed all this, and in the late forties 'a phenomenal interest in

---

[29] 'Put Policy on the Agenda', *op. cit.*, p. 28; Even so, a CLP member complained in the *Manchester
Guardian* two years later (1954): 'What do we talk about? Long and interminable discussions on the
football competition, the Party social, the outing, and the best way of getting the crockery back from the
public hall'.

[30] Milne, R. S., and MacKenzie, H. C., *Marginal Seat 1955*, Hansard Society, 1958.

[31] Birch, A. H., *Small Town Politics: A Study of Political Life in Glossop*, Oxford University Press,
1959, pp. 92–4.

[32] Berry, D., *The Sociology of Grass Roots Politics*, MacMillan, 1970, pp. 46–7.

politics characterized the politics of Newcastle as elsewhere in Britain'.[33]
But this new found enthusiasm for democracy soon gave way to more 'normal' levels of interest. The late forties episode, they say, should be seen as being brought about by exceptional causes rather than as a stage in party development.

A measure of this change is provided by the figures for ward and general management committee attendance. In one ward (and it is in the wards where growth or decline will first manifest itself) attendance rose steadily to peak in 1950, but then fell continuously through the fifties. From an average of 31 in the period 1949–51, GMC attendance was down to 17 in 1959–62. Moreover, the actual number of GMC meetings was also down, as was attendance at annual general meetings.

In 1960–1, although an impressive 39 per cent of all members claimed to have attended a ward meeting in the last two months, very few members appeared to be very active. According to an extremely generous definition of '100 per cent active' (to qualify, all the member had to have done was to help in the local and general election, to have been on a committee in the last ten years, and to have attended a party meeting in the last ten months) only 22 per cent of all members could be so described. Seventy-eight per cent were therefore less than '100 per cent' active.[34] Members were also asked how satisfied they were with the local party and whether they wanted to see any improvements. From their replies, the authors concluded that 'the picture which can be drawn from the suggestions and figures is that the Labour members see themselves as an ageing party in which internal bickering is frequent, and are concerned about inadequate public activity'.[35]

More surprisingly, no less than 54 per cent of the members said that they had never heard of Clause IV of the Party Constitution, despite the fact that the survey was carried out in 1960–1, during the 'Revisionist' debate. However, of those who had heard of it, 57 per cent wanted to keep it as it was. On another two measures of political knowledge – whether the members had heard of the Conference resolution on unilateral disarmament, and whether they knew how the party leader was elected – the replies were 'somewhat disappointing'.[36] Only 26 per cent of the membership had a 'reasonable political knowledge of the Labour Party' in that they knew about these three things.

---

[33] Bealey, *et al.*, pp. 405–6.
[34] *ibid.*, pp. 266–7.
[35] *ibid.*, p. 269.
[36] *ibid.*, p. 284.

As to the content of local party meetings, the authors say much the same
s the authors of the previous studies quoted. They estimate, for instance,
ıat about 60 per cent of the time at general management committee
ıeetings is occupied with constitutional and organizational subjects.
ecause little public activity is carried on between elections, this leads
ıem to suggest that 'the constituency party is primarily organised for elec-
ɔral ends. . . . The emphasis throughout the Party is on building the party
ıachine, gaining new members, and organisational tasks of this nature
ather than on propaganda and public activity.'[37]
The authors conclude by saying that their study of the evolution of New-
ɹastle CLP

> gives a pointer to the conditions in which Constituency Labour Parties
> grow up and flourish. The periods of greatest vitality were in times of
> social upheaval and realignment of attitudes – namely in the turbulent
> social and economic years following the First World War, and the later
> war-time and post-war period of the 1940s, when it had an unparalleled
> increase of growth and influence. . . . For some four years during the
> period 1947–50 there was a well-organised mass Labour Party in New-
> castle, the only time in the four decades of its history that this has
> occurred.[38]

However, they also point out, almost as an afterthought, that 'Labour
entiment remains strong and electoral support high' even though by
960–1 the party was a lot smaller and a lot less active.[39]
On the basis of these studies, we have, therefore three propositions to
ıake concerning participation in local Labour parties which are of special
elevance to the Hindess theory. The first is that membership and par-
icipation levels have always been low but they can rise or fall quite
lramatically in exceptional periods such as the immediate post-war period
.nd during the 1966–70 Labour government. It would however be wholly
vrong to extrapolate long-term declines in participation on the basis of
elatively short-term fluctuations. Second, because the functions of local
₋abour parties have been primarily electoral, and very little activity of a
lirectly political nature is undertaken between elections (except, perhaps,
he passing of resolutions) a significant proportion of participants have
•een attracted into local Labour parties by the residual or secondary

---

[37] *ibid.*, p. 102.
[38] *ibid.*, p. 104.
[39] *ibid.*, p. 105.

'social' function. Third, there appears to be no clear and obvious link between simple participation rates in local Labour parties and the electoral fortunes of the Labour Party. Short-term rises and falls in activity have not always corresponded simply with electoral success or failure for the Labour Party at the national level. The mediations between the Labour Party, its members, its supporters, and the electorate as a whole are more complicated than that.

Changes there may have been, and we now turn to a consideration of two suggested changes – both involving 'decline' – the decline of working class participation in local Labour parties, with its corollary, the 'middle class takeover', and the decline of 'class politics' within local Labour parties. The first 'decline' involves a change of degree, the second involves change of a more qualitative nature.

The Working Class and Local Labour Parties

Two political sociologists recently wrote that the

> studies of political participation . . . have thrown a great deal of light on the linkage between participation and class position, and have made manifest the ways in which the normal operation of the social structure serves to weaken the political effectiveness of movements based on the lower class by reducing the involvement in politics of their potential followers.[40]

The social skills and advantages conferred upon middle and upper class people (higher education, social contacts, etc.) has enabled them to play a disproportionately active part in party political activity, and they have traditionally occupied most of the key positions in the political parties and in government. Attempts to involve more working class people in the political system as a whole have always run up against powerful pressures arising out of the inequality of opportunity built into the social structure.

The rise of the Labour Party, together with the extension of the franchise, brought many hundreds of thousands of working class people into political life who had previously been excluded. It was only through the Labour Party, of course, that working class candidates were first elected to parliament in large numbers. In this sense the Labour Party was

---

[40] Bendix, R., and Lipset, S. M., 'The Field of Political Sociology', in Coser, L. (ed.), *Political Sociology*, Harper, New York, 1966, p. 31.

a considerable achievement – it was the vehicle by which the working class broke through the middle class domination of party politics. But some have argued that the pressures inherent in the social structure are beginning to re-assert themselves ever more strongly, and not only is the PLP becoming more middle class (which it is, though this needs to be qualified, as we have seen) but that the working class are also being squeezed out or are dropping out of local Labour parties. Hindess, for instance, says that there is 'a long-term decline of active Labour support among many sections of the working class'.[41] This is evident, he says, in large urban parties where the strength of Labour's organization in working class areas has been declining, while the relative strength of wards in the middle class areas has been increasing. In consequence, the middle class activists in the middle class wards have come to dominate the local party machinery, and have imposed their own ideas on the local parties, thus further alienating working class supporters. In the process, 'class politics' as such, or 'political activity resulting from identification with, and commitment to, the working class' has also declined, according to Hindess.

This last point is the most difficult to test because we would need to examine all Party leaflets and pamphlets published, every speech made, and ideally, conduct interviews with Labour activists in, say, the 1920s and 1930s to find out their motivations and concerns – but that, clearly, is impossible. But we do have some evidence, and we begin with some evidence on levels of working class participation in local Labour parties.

The authors of the Newcastle-under-Lyme study of 1960–1 found that the local Labour Party was 'indubitably a working class party', and as such was clearly differentiated from other local parties.[42]

Seventy-seven per cent of all Labour Party members were either skilled or less skilled manual workers, 13 per cent were clerical workers, and only 10 per cent fell into the professional/managerial category. These proportions reflected 'fairly closely' the occupational structure of this safe Labour constituency as a whole. Interestingly enough, though only 18 per cent of the local Conservatives were manual workers, because their total membership was nearly four times greater than Labour's, the actual number of manual working class Conservative members was very nearly the same as the number that were in the Labour Party.

While the Newcastle party was thus 'indubitably working class', the authors found that there was some evidence of middle class influence in-

[41] Hindess, B., *The Decline of Working Class Politics*, MacGibbon & Kee, 1971, p. 120.

[42] Bealey, *et al.*, *op. cit.*, pp. 271–2.

creasing. For instance, only three out of thirteen 'stalwart' members in 1949–51 were non manual workers, whereas by 1960–2 five out of eight 'stalwarts' were non-manual. Yet in an earlier historical period the situation was not all that different. We are told, for instance, that the leadership of the local party in the 1920s was predominantly 'lower middle class',[43] and the story of Roberts and Mayer (which provides an interesting sidelight on the role of local Labour parties as a mechanism of social mobility) tends to corroborate the argument that all was not glorious socialist struggle in those days:

> In 1925, Ellis Roberts, a railwayman, became the first Labour Mayor. Social elevation also accompanied civic distinction. By the late 1920s Roberts had become a coal merchant while Mayer, Labour's first pioneer (elected as a bricklayer and first Labour Councillor in 1905) was a builder and a Ratepayer's Councillor.[44]

Other surveys have produced varying conclusions. A study of South West Wales in the early 1950s found that the leadership of the local Labour parties was trade union dominated and 'overwhelmingly working class' – 79 per cent were so classified. But they also found that the few middle class members around participated to a much greater degree in party activity. Moreover, most of the children of the local trade union and party leaders were not only going into middle class occupations, but most were no longer associated with the Labour movement at all.[45] The Fabian sample survey of nine Manchester ward parties found that there was very little difference in activity rates of members in different social classes. Only 12 per cent of the members in the sample were middle class, and in no type of activity of office-holding did they account for more than 14 per cent of the total. But in more detailed study of one working class ward they found that middle class and lower middle class members accounted for only 6 per cent of the total membership but 29 per cent of the meeting-attenders.[46] Birch, in his study of local politics in Glossop, also found that the middle classes were much more active in the local Labour Party. While industrial workers accounted for 77 per cent of the Labour voters and 76 per cent of the Labour members, only 33 per cent of the local Labour 'leaders' were industrial workers. Thirty-four per cent of the local Labour 'leaders' were either

[43] *ibid.*, p. 34.

[44] *ibid.*, p. 46.

[45] Brennan, T., Cooney, E. W., and Pollins, H., *Social Change in South West Wales,* Watts, 1954, pp. 170–1.

[46] 'Put Policy on the Agenda', *op. cit.*, pp. 28–9.

business proprietors or professional/managerial workers, but these groups only accounted for 5 per cent of the Labour voters and only 7 per cent of the Labour members.[47] Similarly, a much bigger survey of local Labour leaders in thirty-six constituencies by Janosik – the sample included MPs and prospective parliamentary candidates – also found that only 26 per cent were skilled or semi-skilled workers, while 32 per cent were businessmen or professionals. Younger leaders, though few in number, tended to be better educated and more middle class – perhaps an augury for the future.[48]

Membership of local authorities is one level of political participation at which the middle classes have traditionally been over-represented. Elected councillors have nearly always been more middle class than the population as a whole. G. W. Jones, in his historical study of politics in Wolverhampton, found that the percentage of 'workers' (compared with professionals, white collar workers, women and retired persons) never exceeded 10 per cent before 1919, was only around 16 or 17 per cent between the wars, and was still only 18 per cent in the period 1950–60.[49] One or two specific councils – like 1945–6 and 1953–4 – reported higher proportions temporarily (the maximum was 25 per cent) and recruits in the Labour 'heyday' period of 1945–53 were 31 per cent working class. But even this proportion had fallen to 15 per cent in the period 1953–62. Working class representation in this sense therefore reached a peak in the late 1940s and early 1950s, and has since levelled-off or dropped slightly.

A larger study by L. J. Sharpe of the socio-economic background of councillors on thirteen County Councils and seventeen County Borough Councils around 1960 found that local government was massively dominated by the middle classes, with almost no unskilled workers anywhere. However, when he looked at changes between 1930 and 1959 in a smaller study of three Councils – Kent County Council, Croydon County Borough Council and the Borough of Lewisham – the only 'really substantial change' was a steady increase since 1930 in the proportion of working class members elected. But even so, when 'routine non-manual' workers were included in the 'working class' category, this only accounted for 11 per cent of the elected councillors in Kent, 36 per cent in Croydon, and 50 per cent in Lewisham.[50] A similar survey by the same author of the 1961

---

[47] Birch, *op. cit.*, pp. 66–7 and p. 81.

[48] Janosik, E. G., *Constituency Labour Parties in Britain*, Pall Mall, 1968, pp. 9–25.

[49] Jones, G. W., *Borough Politics: A Study of the Wolverhampton Town Council 1888–1964*, Macmillan, 1969.

[50] Sharpe, L. J., 'Elected Representatives in Local Government', *British Journal of Sociology*, 1962, vol. 13, pp. 189–208.

London County Council elections revealed that 52 per cent of the Labour candidates elected were in non-manual 'middle class' occupations and only 21 per cent were in manual 'working class' occupations.[51]

Confirmation that this phenomena of middle class over-representation extends into safe Labour areas is provided in Hampton's Sheffield study. The description of candidates on ballot papers were analysed for selected periods over the past forty years, and it was found that the proportion of Labour councillors who were manual workers had declined slightly from 40 per cent in 1926 (and 32 per cent in 1936) to 29 per cent in 1967. The proportion of white collar Labour councillors had increased from 5 to 24 per cent, and professionals from 3 to 11 per cent. But, if we bear in mind that the increase in white collar Labour councillors has been mainly at the expense of full-time Trade Union officials and Party Agents, then the occupational composition of the Labour Group has not changed all that much over the past forty years. And even in 1967–8, it was still the case that two thirds of all Labour councillors had been only to elementary or secondary modern schools, so a fair number of the white collar members were in origin 'working class'. Nevertheless as Hampton himself points out, 'it is surprising to discover that even in an industrial city like Sheffield a minority of Labour councillors came from manual occupations'.[52]

So it is fairly true to say that middle class people have always been disproportionately more active in local community affairs, and that this includes participation in local Labour parties and membership of Labour groups on local authorities. One might also say that, on the whole, the nature of their work and their educational background endows middle class people with certain social skills which make it easier for them to participate in voluntary organizations like local Labour parties. But, in the case of local Labour parties, this is probably nothing very new, and it is not clear whether there is an identifiable 'trend' in differential participation rates at all. The lack of evidence, and the problems of assessing evidence based on different 'classifications' of people makes it difficult, if not impossible, to draw any firm conclusions as to whether 'working class' participation in local Labour parties is going up or coming down. What we can say is that it is extremely doubtful that there has been a recent and extensive working class exit from local Labour parties, as Hindess suggests.

As to the other propositions in the Hindess argument, evidence for and against them is even more scanty (though their logic should also be

---

[51] Sharpe, L. J., *A Metropolis Votes, op. cit.*, pp. 29–42.
[52] Hampton, *op. cit.*, p. 189.

questioned). In relation to the suggestion that middle class wards have become stronger than working class wards, there are two studies which contain relevant data. Gould's survey of 'Riverside' CLP in the early 1950s found that what he called the 'working class wards' were stronger in terms of membership than the 'middle class wards'. The latter had an average membership of 214, while the five 'working class wards' had an average of 318 members each.[53] But Blondel, in a study of the Labour Party in Reading, found otherwise. He traced the history of the CLP – which, incidentally, was second in size only to Woolwich in the 1920s – and found the 'normal' pattern of development – low membership and little activity in the 1930s, a post-war upswing in activity peaking in 1950, and a subsequent return to lower levels of activity. Even more interesting, he found that those wards he defined as 'middle class' were strongest in the pre-war years. He cites the results of a 1936 financial appeal which showed that seven ward associations in middle class Tory wards (all of which contained less than 10 per cent of Labour electors) had 41 per cent of all CLP members and contributed 72 per cent of the appeal money.[54] Four working class wards with most of the Labour vote had only 59 per cent of the members and contributed only 28 per cent of the appeal money. But – and this is an important point – he says that even this apparent disparity in strength could merely be accounted for by 'historical' or 'accidental' reasons – such as the presence of one or two particularly active individuals or families who happen to have moved into one ward rather than another. The relatively greater strength of middle class wards in some areas in some periods does not therefore appear to be something entirely new. Moreover, Baxter, in his own study of politics in Liverpool, directly challenges the very basis of Hindess' theory. He concludes:

It seems from all the evidence that is available that the organisation of the Labour Party in Liverpool had always been bad apart from occasional exceptions. . . . There is no evidence at all that the parties were any stronger in the mainly working-class constituencies such as Edge Hill, Exchange, Kirkdale, or Scotland, at any time during the last forty years. It is very easy to argue that the parties in these constituencies were weaker in 1970 than in 1960 but that can quite reasonably be explained by the decline in Labour morale and fortunes during the

---

[53] Gould, *op. cit.*

[54] Blondel, J., 'The Conservative Association and the Labour Party in Reading', *Political Studies*, 1958, vol. VI, no. 2, pp. 101–119.

1967–9 period, and it would not seem unreasonable to expect the situation to change during the early nineteen-seventies.[55]

In relation to the second proposition that there has been a decline of 'class politics' *per se*, that Labour activity rooted in 'identification with, and commitment to, the working class as such' has declined, Baxter says that the Liverpool Labour Party, and especially the membership of the Labour group on the City Council, was always made-up of non-socialists who 'were not in politics for class reasons at all'.[56] Many Labour activists and leaders, he says, were more interested in the social prestige and status of being a councillor than with waging class war or introducing class politics into the Council Chamber. It is, therefore, rather difficult to speak of a 'decline' in 'class politics' in Liverpool – even if we could agree on a definition – when there wasn't much 'class politics' in the Labour Party in the first place. There was nothing to 'decline' from.

There is, however, some evidence to suggest that the political concerns and orientations of middle class Labour activists differ from those of the working class activists. For instance, the Fabian CLP study mentioned above suggested that the political attitudes of middle class members were likely to be more 'idealist' and less 'down-to-earth' in that they were more concerned with intangible issues like foreign policy, whereas working class members were more concerned with issues like housing conditions, issues which affected them in their everyday lives. Hindess, too, pointed up housing as a key issue on which a different level of interest is shown by different sections of the membership.

All this would seem to be intuitively correct, and it is certainly true to say that it is the middle class radicals who frequently show more interest in policy areas like transportation, planning and the environment, but though firm evidence either way is lacking, it is extremely doubtful that 'working class issues' like housing and social services are being ignored by local Labour parties, at least not to the extent that Hindess suggests.[57] And it would be illogical to say that there has been a decline of 'class politics' *because* more members and leaders of local Labour parties are drawn from higher socio-economic groups, even if the latter statement is correct. The extent of the practice of 'class politics' is determined by many other factors,

---

[55] Baxter, R., 'The Working Class and Labour Politics', *Political Studies*, 1972, vol. XX, no. 1, p. 105.

[56] *ibid.*, p. 106.

[57] However, there is some evidence to suggest that the house-building records of Labour controlled London boroughs are hardly better than Conservative-held boroughs. See Richard Minns, 'Who Builds More?', *New Society*, 25 Apr. 1974.

especially ideological ones. There is no *simple or causal* relationship between the promulgation of class politics and the socio-economic group of the individual doing it. Just as 'working class' Labour councillors can be reactionaries, personally motivated by concerns other than the interests of the working class, so too can 'middle class' councillors be radical class crusaders, personally motivated by an ideological commitment to 'the working class as such'. In short, there is not enough empirical evidence to validate the decline of working class politics/middle class takeover argument, and in any case, it is illogical in certain crucial senses.

Working Class Communities and the 'Golden Past'

A fourth suggestion is that local Labour parties are becoming increasingly irrelevant to their local electorate and supporters, partly because they play no real role in the local community (except at election times), and partly because they are not dealing with the issues that concern people, especially working class people. Hindess writes:

> the fact that the issues themselves are increasingly raised outside the formal political organisations (by tenant's associations, squatters, community action and Far Left groups etc.). . . . marks the breakdown of that social control which the Labour Party has been able to exercise over such a large section of the population.[58]

This raises the question of what precisely is or was the 'social control' that the Labour Party has exercised or exercises over its working class supporters, but once again, the assumption behind the above statement is that there has been a decline – indeed, 'breakdown' – and that things were somehow much better in the past than they are today. The implication is that in the old days the local Labour party supported more local activity and played a much greater role in the community, especially in local working class communities, and that working class people in particular were much more likely to turn to the Labour Party for assistance. Contemporary local Labour parties are seen as a palid version of their former selves.

All this, too, is extremely dubious, and contains most of the 'golden past' myths that I have been anxious to dispel in preceding chapters of this book. What evidence we do have suggests that there is unlikely to have been

---

[58] Hindess, *op. cit.*, p. 172.

much of a 'breakdown in social control' because there was not much 'social control' – beyond habitual electoral allegiance – in the first place. As we saw in Chapter Two, electoral habits die hard, and there has been no obvious breakdown of Labour's *electoral* 'social control'. Whether there has been a significant change in the *meaning* of voting Labour is a different matter.

Nor is it likely that issues are *increasingly* raised outside formal political organizations like the Labour Party. There has always been a proliferation of political groupings and one-issue campaigns on the periphery of the Labour Party. For years the ILP played an important role, long after it had left the official Party, and even Hindess' squatting is not an entirely new phenomena. There was, it is true, an increase in all kinds of extra-Labour Party socialist activity during the period 1966–70, much of which continued despite suggestions that it would decline as soon as Labour was back in Opposition, but whether any *new* significance can be attached to these groups and activities is more difficult to assess.

The 'breakdown of Labour's social control' aspect of the argument is important because it not only presupposes that local Labour parties played a much more significant role in working class communities in the past, it also poses the problem of the 'working class community' itself – was it, too, a myth? Did it really exist, and if so, in what senses? Or is it just another nostalgic, romantic, notion?[59] Did it really play an important part in the development – or restriction – of radical working class consciousness?

First of all, it must be said that there has been a definite tendency to over-romanticize the 'working class community', and to freely use the term without really examining what it means. Seabrook, for example is one writer who has implicitly cast doubt on the 'romantic' view of the traditional working class community. In his literary account of a working class street over the last hundred years, he emphasizes over again the restricting role of the 'rigidly fixed patterns of behaviour and relationships',[60] and provides a very bitter account of the prevailing insularity, apathy, rivalry, superstition, deference, racialism, the unquestioning acceptance of ancient beliefs, the victimization of deviants, and a general absence of neighbourliness in this working class 'community'. But a most relevant and interesting study of life in a working class community is provided by Robert Roberts in *The Classic Slum*, a first-

---

[59] See Wood, M., on 'Nostalgia', *New Society*, 7 Nov. 1974.
[60] Seabrook, J., *The Unprivileged*, Penguin, 1973, p. 159.

hand account of his boyhood experiences in Salford in the first quarter of this century.[61]

Roberts is particularly keen to emphasize the role of stratification *within* the working class. There was, he says, a class structure within the working class which divided neighbour from neighbour, worker from worker – a kind of 'English proletarian caste system'.[62] But this class structure was based not so much on economic categories, more on morals and 'respectability'. For instance, he reveals how the common family feuds would frequently erupt into shouting matches in the street, even public violence, and as a result the doorstep matriarchs would make 'grim readjustments on the social ladder'.[63] The reality of 'working class community' life, he says, was much harsher and much more unpleasant than many contemporary writers (who have probably never lived in one) like to make out. He criticizes those authors who sentimentalize and caricature the working class, adding:

> In our day some sociologists have been apt to write fondly about the cosy gregariousness of the old slum dwellers. Their picture, I think, has been overdrawn. Close propinquity, together with cultural poverty, led as much to emnity as it did to friendship. . . . People deprived of social outlets only too easily gave over their minds to the affairs of others. . . . In general, slum life was far from being the jolly hive of communal activity that some romantics have claimed.[64]

He continues (in a direct reference to myths of the 'golden past'):

> Some professional inquirers into the past have persuaded the elderly both to reminisce and to complete lengthy questionnaires covering aspects of their lives in youth. This can of course yield valuable information, social and historical. But a certain caution is needed. During the '30s and '40s I often talked with people who were already mature by 1914. They criticised the then fairly recent past, faculties alert, with what seemed some objectivity. But by the 60s, myths had developed, prejudices about the present had set hard; these same critics, in ripe old age, now saw the Edwardian era through a golden haze![65]

Miliband, as we have seen, has argued that many people see the socialist

---

[61] Roberts, R., *The Classic Slum – Salford Life in the First Quarter of the Century*, Pelican, 1973.
[62] *ibid.*, p. 13.
[63] *ibid.*, p. 24.
[64] *ibid.*, pp. 47 and 49.
[65] *ibid.*, footnote p. 25.

movement of the late nineteenth century, the immediately pre-First World War, and the interwar periods in a similar light.[66] My point is that this may be part of a general phenomenon, perhaps a fundamental psychological process, and that local Labour parties of earlier times, too, are often viewed through a 'golden haze'. Perhaps they weren't as thriving and as significant as former activists would have us believe. Certainly, the fragmentary evidence we do have suggests that this is most probably the case.

In fact, Roberts has quite a bit to say about the role of politics in the working class community as well, including some trenchant comments on the significance of the Salford-based, Marxist, Social Democratic Federation:

> The first of our public buildings reared its dark bulk near the railway wall. Hyndman Hall, home of the Social Democratic Federation, remained mysteriously aloof and through the years had, in fact, about as much political impact on the neighbourhood as the nearby gasworks. The second establishment, our Conservative Club, except for a few days at election times, didn't appear to meddle with politics at all. It was notable usually for a union jack in the window and a brewer's dray at the door.[67]

According to Roberts, the failure of socialist ideology to make an impact in any form continued right up until 1914. In spite of the Clarion movement propaganda, the million copies of *Merrie England* sold, and the growing strength of the Labour Party, socialism had little appeal for the lower working class – although the trade unions were making quiet, but steady progress. When socialist speakers did visit the slum, their reception was hardly ecstatic:

> Marxist 'ranters' from the Hall who paid fleeting visits to our street end insisted that we, the proletariat, stood locked in titanic struggle with some wicked master class. We were battling, they told us (from a vinegar barrel borrowed from our corner shop), to cast off our chains and win a whole world. Most people passed by; a few stood to listen, but not for long: the problems of the 'proletariat', they felt, had little to do with them.[68]

The class struggle was recognized, not in any way as a war against the

---

[66] Miliband, 'Socialism and the Myth of the Golden Past', in *Socialist Register 1964*, Merlin Press, 1964.

[67] Roberts, *op. cit.*, pp. 16–17.

[68] *ibid.*, p. 28.

employers, but 'a series of engagements in the battle of life itself'.[69] Deference among the lower orders was so ingrained that it seemed that 'the less they had to conserve the more conservative in spirit they showed themselves.'[70] Wages were accepted gratefully from 'kind' employers, and by voting Conservative they felt 'at one' with them.

It was the First World War – Roberts calls it 'the Great Release' – which did so much to erode traditional attitudes of deference, and to create a new confidence among the lower orders, disenchanted with their 'betters'. Even so, foreign events like the Russian Revolution were barely noticed in the Salford Slum:

> In our small grey purlieu of the industrial North we heard indifferently about the Russian Revolution, only perking up interest at the news of 'cannibalism among the reds'. A few strange un-English names lodged for a time in our consciousness. Among a litter of pups, Mrs. Woods, the butcher's wife, had a pair which she called Lenin and Trotsky. We laughed. Russia was no concern of ours.[71]

But the domestic experience of war, the new freedoms and the higher wages, led to a rapid increase in unionization and support for the Labour Party. Marxism still failed to take a hold, and Roberts recalls

> a course which opened with fanfare and fifty four students in a room over the bar at the local trades club, to study (under a man with a large red beard) the 'first nine chapters of *Das Kapital*'. After a month only three of us remained ... This class was the prototype of innumerable similar fiascos which occurred right through the '20s.[72]

Yet all the time electoral support for the Labour Party was growing. Although Roberts never attempts an appraisal of the kind and quality of the loyalty enjoyed by the Labour Party at this time (which is a great pity), he does give us a glimpse of the feelings of temporary euphoria engendered by the Labour gains in the General Election of 1924: 'On the night of that triumph, our Constituency returned it's first Labour MP, simple socialists like my mother wept for joy and we, the young, felt ourselves the heralds of a new age.'[73]

---

[69] *ibid.*, p. 28.
[70] *ibid.*, p. 167.
[71] *ibid.*, p. 214.
[72] *ibid.*, p. 220.
[73] *ibid.*, p. 221.

One's first reaction to this description is to say that sort of thing would not happen today. I cannot be certain whether anyone wept for joy on election night in, say, 1945 – I suspect that quite a few did. People often do that kind of thing on election night. In fact, I vividly remember watching a Labour candidate, his family, and a number of supporters crying their eyes out on the night a London constituency went Labour for the first time in 1964 – and many of us youngsters certainly thought that we were on the verge of a new age. So I don't think we can hang too much on that piece of evidence, but it does raise once again the problem of assessing qualitative changes in Labour loyalty, the flavour of working class politics, and the *meaning* of working class and Labour politics to the participants. We shall return to the problem of qualitative change in our concluding comments.

Parkin argues explicitly that the 'one class' working class community – such as it is, or was – has usually acted as a barrier to the development of a radical working class class-consciousness. We saw in the discussion of Labour Party 'thought' that Parkin distinguishes three kinds of 'value system' – the 'dominant', the 'subordinate' and the 'radical'. The 'subordinate' value system, he says, is essentially *accommodative* towards the existing system of social relations, representing neither endorsement nor outright opposition to the status quo. It is based on the working class community, and working class communities have traditionally inhibited the extension of the 'radical' value system:

> They generate a meaning system which is of purely parochial significance, representing a design for living based upon localised social knowledge and face-to-face relationships. A class outlook, on the other hand, is rooted in a perception of the social order that stretches far beyond the frontier of community. It entails a macro-social view of the reward structure and some understanding of the systematic nature of inequality. In a way, becoming class conscious, at least in the ideal-typical sense, could be likened to learning a foreign language: that is, it presents men with a new vocabulary and a new set of concepts which permit a different translation of the meaning of inequality from that encouraged by the conventional vocabulary of society.[74]

Similarly, Mann has argued that 'there is no *need* for working class people to develop beliefs which legitimate or illegitimate society, as long as they recognise the *factual* need to comply with its demands. Only those

---

[74] Parkin, F., *Class Inequality and Political Order*, MacGibbon & Kee, 1971, p. 90.

who seek to change society need to encompass it intellectually'.[75] And others have also argued that the manifestation of feelings of 'relative deprivation' (or dissatisfaction with one's lot relative to others) on the part of working class people has been restricted by the one-class nature of working class communities. Geographical proximity and social interaction means that working class people in working class communities tend to take as their reference group other members of the same class – they do not always compare their 'lot' with members of other, more privileged classes.

On the other hand, it could be argued that working class communities have played an important role in cementing certain forms of local solidarity – such as electoral allegiance to the Labour Party. It is known, for instance, that neighbourhood pressures play a part in determining voting behaviour and such influences in the 'one class' working class communities tend to increase the proportion voting Labour among the inhabitants. Modern council estates are an example of this phenomena. The whole problem of the political implications of the working class community therefore needs to be further explored. But just as the consensus at a recent SSRC conference on the 'traditional worker' agreed that it was very difficult to say whether and in what senses the 'traditional worker' does or did exist, and that everything is much more complex and heterogeneous than even social scientists tend to think, so too must the concept of the 'working class community' itself be treated with circumspection. Parkin's scheme may be superficially attractive, but we must bear in mind – as Lockwood said in concluding the SSRC conference – that 'social life has an obdurate complexity which can be counted upon (fortunately) to badly dent, if not demolish, most sociological concepts that are unlucky enough to make contact with it'.[76]

Labour and the Local Community

Finally I would like to comment on some possible reasons why Constituency Labour Parties have only played a limited role in the local community, and suggestions that the traditional electoral activities of the local organizations of the mass parties have now been superceded by electioneering via the mass media.

---

[75] Mann, M., 'The Ideologies of Non-Skilled Industrial Workers' in *Proceedings of the Social Science Research Council Conference: The Occupational Community of the Traditional Worker*, Durham, 1973, p. 272.

[76] Lockwood, *op. cit.*, p. 445.

First, in relation to the limited role of CLPs, it should be noted that CLPs and their ward associations are based on *electoral* boundaries. The geographical area covered by each ward and constituency is an electoral division. It does not necessarily coincide with existing 'communities' – even assuming that we could agree on how to define where each 'community' begins and ends. Nor, as Hampton points out, is there any evidence to suggest that ward boundaries can *create* a community or a community consciousness.[77] Artificial electoral divisions are therefore a major constraint on all political parties attempting to play a significant role in the local community.

In fact, Hampton took the analysis one stage further in his Sheffield study, because he found that even the existence of social 'communities' did not predetermine the existence of political 'communities'. Surprisingly, 'neighbourhood attachment' was *not* related to 'interest in local affairs': 'the distinction must be made', he wrote, 'between a community in a social – almost anthropological – sense, and a political community.'[78] In other words, a close-knit community of long-term residents might exist, with extensive kinship networks and interpersonal contacts, and yet political involvement may be negligible, or it may be considerable. Even the existence of 'community' cannot predict political involvement.

Second, because CLPs are rarely deep-rooted in the local community, and because they are forced to operate within artificial boundaries, this means that most elected councillors are not 'community leaders' in any real sense at all. Again, Hampton found this in the Labour areas of Sheffield: 'The majority of councillors are not community leaders who emerge from the wards they represent; they are people interested in public affairs who seek an opportunity to represent their fellow citizens wherever it may conveniently be found'.[79]

Non-resident councillors are less likely to appreciate the problems of their ward, and are less likely to be available or to have frequent social contacts with their constituents. This further diminishes the prospects of the local party developing into a major community institution, voicing the wishes and concerns of the local community.

It also introduces a third factor which could be seen as a third stage in the process or vicious circle, not of decline, but of the non-development of local Labour parties into major community institutions. Because few coun-

---

[77] Hampton, *Democracy and Community, op. cit.*

[78] *ibid.*, p. 121.

[79] *ibid.*, p. 203.

cillors emerge out of their wards as 'community leaders' – and more often than not they are a kind of 'allotment holder', given a 'patch' in return for services rendered – this further militates against greater activity and involvement because the elected councillor's reference group is the local political community and not the local community itself. The local *political* community is made up of all those who are active in official local politics – usually elected councillors or officers of the political parties. In the words of Hampton: '. . . they meet each other regularly, share common interests, and denounce public apathy towards their activities with a vehemence only matched by the suspicion they sometimes evidence towards those who seek to contest their authority.'[80] It is this group to whom the newly-elected councillor owes his allegiance, and from whom he takes his cues. Because there is no *community control* over the councillor, there is no *need* for him or her to independently champion local causes. Provided the councillor does not fall out with the local political community or with the few active members of his ward association, his or her position is a relatively safe one. Obviously if the seat is electorally marginal the councillor will have to pay a little more attention to constituency work between elections, but if the seat is 'safe', then accountability to the community is negligible. From the elected councillor's point of view, there is no real *need* to develop the ward association into an effective community institution – provided the vote can be got out at the appropriate time.

Associated with this is the problem of the kind of people who become councillors and the reasons why they wish to become councillors. We turn to Baxter for a description taken from his observations of elected representatives in Liverpool:

> It is important to remember that a man may go onto a Council to do something, he may also go on to be someone. Membership of the Council carries with it some social prestige, but possibly more important is the prestige it brings to a councillor in his own eyes – the satisfaction of feeling important. All the trapping of civic pomp encourage this, from the debates in the Council Chamber, which can involve large sums of money, to membership of the Parks and Gardens Committee, with its official dinners and tours of inspection, and well-paid senior officials of the city being polite and helpful to working men who may well get no respect or satisfaction in their everyday lives. To them politics offers an escape, and the personal satisfaction that can be derived from the forms

---

80 Hampton, *op. cit.*, p. 49.

of local government could be enough to leave them uninterested in the substance of policy matters.[81]

In the section on local Labour Parties, I suggested that the relationships between the Labour Party, its members, supporters and the electorate at large are complicated, and levels of participation in local Labour parties were not simply related to the electoral fortunes of the party. This is obvious because there were times, like the early fifties and the late fifties/early sixties, when participation levels were high, but electoral success eluded the Party. Party *morale* seems to be the key factor influencing participation, and the post-war experience suggests that this is primarily (though not solely) related to the perceived performance of the Labour Party in power. By and large, Labour supporters were reasonably pleased with the 1945–50 performance, and they continued to work for the Party. In 1966–70, the activists and members, disillusioned with the Labour government, left the Party in their thousands. But who could say that Labour's By-Election and municipal election disasters during 1966–70 were simply caused by the exit of the activists who manned the polling stations and committee rooms, or that the activists simply left *because* of the electoral defeats? The reality of the situation was obviously more complicated, but it is most likely that the majority of the electorate were disenchanted by a perceived poor showing in the Government's handling of the economy, while the party's activists were disenchanted by the lack of progress in a socialist direction, and both factors— electoral popularity and 'internal' party morale – reacted upon each other to produce catastrophic results. But some have argued implicitly that the views of the members and activists are becoming less and less relevant as the local parties themselves become less and less relevant in the electioneering process.

The argument is an attractive one: mainly because TV ownership has spread, electioneering is now conducted almost entirely through the national media, and sophisticated market research enables the party leaderships to assess the mood of the voters far more accurately than any canvass returns. As McKenzie put it in 1955:

> there is much evidence to support the view that the traditional electoral activities of the mass party, including the conduct of public meetings, canvassing and the rest, are now of declining importance in influencing the outcome of elections. It seems likely that the really effective elec-

---

[81] *ibid.*, p. 106.

tioneering of the future will rely increasingly on the newer mass media of radio, and, above all, of television.[82]

Similarly, Beer was argued that:

> Broadly, the effect of the new technology is to enable central units to by-pass intermediary levels and directly to assess and influence voters' opinions. This could mean a shift of important functions, and therefore power, from local parties to the central offices. . . . If the new technology continues to shift function to central agencies, the local parties, and especially the local activists, will decline in importance. Conceivably in time, a new kind of technocratic cadre party could take the place of the familiar mass party . . .

However, he adds that 'At present, we are a long way from that eventuality. There are still important functions for local parties and still enough class feeling to provide activists to perform them'.[83]

As a matter of fact, people have been predicting the end of the mass party for decades. And in the 1920s, the Lynds, for instance, in their famous study of Middletown (USA) also suggested that 'declining' interest in political participation was due to new forms of *entertainment* – the movies, radio and commercial sports.[84] It would have seemed plausible to say this about Britain at the time, but, as we have seen, the evidence on turnout and participation does not really bear this out. In fact, it could be argued that the public at large are now *more* exposed to political argument and debate, and are more aware of political issues precisely because of the development of the mass media.

The argument in support of the declining importance of local parties and of local electioneering is based primarily on the assumption that local campaigns now have little influence on the result of elections, yet evidence either way from studies that have been done remains inconclusive. But evidence showing the amount of campaigning actually being done suggests that there has, indeed, been a marked decline in recent years. The Nuffield election studies of 1959, 1964, 1966 and 1970 cite Gallup Poll and National Opinion Poll data which shows that the percentage of the electorate who said that they had been 'approached' by a political party during the campaign fell from 50 per cent in 1959, to 38 per cent in 1964, to 31 per cent in 1966, and 29 per cent in 1970. Moreover, the percentage of Labour voters

[82] McKenzie, *op. cit.*, p. 648.

[83] Beer, S., *Modern British Politics*, Faber, 1969 (2nd edn.), p. 419.

[84] Lynd, R. S. and Lynd, H. M., *Middletown*, New York, 1929, pp. 416–20.

who said that they had been contacted fell even more dramatically from 4
per cent in 1959, to 23 per cent in 1964, 28 per cent in 1966 and to a mere 1
per cent in 1970.[85] Similarly, using Gallup, ORC and NOP data they show
that the proportion who said that they had attended a public meeting
during the campaign had also declined – though only from around 10 per
cent in 1959 to around 6 per cent in 1970.[86]

It may, therefore, be the case that electioneering at the local level is
becoming less important in determining the outcome of national elections
– though this says nothing about local elections, the other half of a local
party's work. But the outcome of national elections are, of course, deter
mined by many other factors, one of which is the morale of the Party
faithful which reacts upon, and in turn is reacted upon, by the electorate at
large. Internal party morale as a whole is still very much dependent on the
contentment of the grass roots activists, and failure to recognize their
feelings can have appalling consequences – as the experience of 1966–70
showed.

Moreover, as long as internal party morale remains an important factor
in party politics, the grass roots will not lose such ability that they may
have had to influence the party leaders – even if their functional role is
declining in some respects.

---

[85] Butler and Rose (1959), p. 140; Butler and King (1964), p. 220; Butler and King (1966), p. 197;
Butler and Pinto-Duschinsky (1970), p. 317.
[86] Butler and Pinto-Duschinsky, *op. cit.*, p. 314.

5. A Constituency Labour Party

Introduction

In 1973, I decided to take four of the main conclusions of Hindess (see page 28 above) at face value, to examine whether the processes he outlined were in fact occurring in a major County Borough. Hindess himself had suggested that we should expect to find similar processes to those allegedly identified in Liverpool occurring in different parts of the country,[1] and even though the Liverpool study had already been subjected to some pretty ruthless criticism,[2] I nevertheless decided that certain of the questions raised by that study were so important, and similar assertions so prevalent that they needed further examination. In addition, putting the Hindess arguments to the 'test' in the Brighton context would give structure to what could otherwise become a rambling survey of 'everything found out in a study of a Constituency Labour Party' – an outcome I wished to avoid.

The first of the four conclusions examined involved the alleged decline in electoral turnout and participation in local Labour parties. The second and third both involved the alleged changing relationship between party and class – the first of these being a progressive decline of activity resulting from identification with the 'working class' as such, the second involving a 'middle class takeover' of local Labour parties. The fourth main conclusion, the alleged breakdown of Labour's traditional 'social control', proved more difficult to 'test'. Although relevant questions were included in a questionnaire to all current members, an analysis of this problem utilizing data from the questionnaire replies did not prove to be feasible,

---

[1] See, for instance, pp. 18 and 132 of *The Decline of Working Class Politics, op. cit.*, and Seyd, P., Review of Hindess in *Bulletin of the Society for the Study of Labour History*, 1972, no. 24, pp. 82–85.

[2] For example, Baxter, R., 'The Working Class and Labour Politics', *Political Studies*, 1972, vol. XX, no. 1, pp. 97–107.

and I was unable to put into operation a testing of this proposition using other methods owing to the constraints under which I was working.

Accurate data relevant to the first three conclusions was generated with greater facility by means of a questionnaire administered to all 927 members (and non-resident Councillors) of the Brighton-Kemptown CLP between 19 July and 18 September 1973. Members' names were drawn from the 1972 or 1973 Ward membership lists, whichever was available. An overall response rate of 61 per cent was achieved, and full details of the survey method appear in Appendix A at the end of the book.[3]

Kemptown was 'chosen' for study simply because I lived there, I knew the area, and I was particularly interested in studying my local party. In this I take comfort from Bernard Crick who recently wrote that 'the study of politics is not something remote from the political process, it must be part of it. And it is not dull or unimaginative to study one's own backyard.'[4] However, a retrospective justification could be made out for choosing Kemptown based on the following: First, Kemptown Constituency itself is both politically marginal and is also reasonably typical of the country as a whole in terms of key social indicators such as the proportion of the electorate in different socio-economic groups. In fact, it is only on car ownership and the proportion of retired persons that Kemptown differs markedly from the national mean:

	% of non-manual (economically active males)	% of professional/ managerial (economically active males)	% of owner-occupier households	% of council tenant households	% of dwellings with full plumbing	% of households with cars	% of population with New Commonwealth roots	% of Young Voters in Electorate	% of population over 65
Kemptown	31·8	12·6	42·6	28·7	75·4	38·9	1·2	10·2	18·1
National average	32·6	15·3	51·4	27·3	73·1	50·8	0·6	10·2	13·0
Rank Ordering	50–	40–	30–	50–		20–	60–	50–	90–
of Kemptown	60%	50%	40%	60%	50%	30%	70%	60%	100%

For instance, according to these figures taken from the Registrar-General's 1961 and 1971 Census data,[5] Kemptown has one of the highest

---

[3] A fairly full account of the results of this survey first appeared in a different form in the *New Statesman* under the title 'Anatomy of a Local Labour Party' on September 28 and October 5, 1973.

[4] Crick, B., in Foreword to Hampton, *Democracy and Community*, Oxford University Press, 1970, p. xxi.

[5] See Butler, D., and Pinto-Duschinsky, M., *The British General Election of 1970*, Macmillan, 1971 (appendix), and Butler, D., and Kavanagh, D., *The British General Election of February 1974*, Macmillan, 1974 (appendix).

oportions of retired people in the country, and over 90 per cent of all con-
tituencies have a lower proportion of retired persons than Kemptown. But
is rank ordering is, in a sense, a little over-dramatic in that the difference
etween the Kemptown figure and the national mean is only around five
er cent. Differences on most other indices are smaller or less significant.

Second, in terms of total membership and activity Kemptown CLP is
kely to be above the national average for CLPs. Earlier I quoted evidence
ggesting that the real membership of CLPs averaged less than 400.
emptown CLPs real membership is between 800 and 900 and it also has
ne of the 120 or so full-time Agents. We can therefore assume that
hatever is found in Kemptown, most CLPs are probably in a worse state
terms of levels of activity.

Third, Kemptown provides something of a critical sample in another
nse. It is now over ten years since the University of Sussex was founded
Brighton, and the campus is located on the boundary of Kemptown
onstituency. Brighton also has a comparatively new Polytechnic and
eacher Training College, apart from an expanded Technical College.
hese developments have resulted in an influx of academic and teaching
affs into the area. In addition, the progressive 'gentrification' of some
aditional working class areas in Kemptown has slightly increased the
roportion of middle class voters in the electorate and has brought young
iddle class couples into certain areas of the constituency. If, therefore, it
argued that new middle class elements are taking over local Labour par-
es – and from the evidence we have of the changing character of the
arliamentary Labour Party, it is the teachers and lecturers who make up
he bulk of the new 'middle class' Labour Members of Parliament – then
emptown would seem to be an appropriate place to test such an argu-
ent. Even though Kemptown is in the 'Deep South' and of course the
emptown CLP is not a City Party like Liverpool (and we know that City
arties have always done particularly badly in terms of levels of par-
cipation), if a 'middle class takeover' is occurring nationwide, then we
ould expect it to show up in a place like Kemptown.

I do not claim that the study of Kemptown Labour Party – based sub-
tantially on a questionnaire administered to current members in 1973 –
epresents a definitive 'test' of the Hindess 'thesis' – or even of the three
tatements taken from Hindess mentioned above. This is mainly because it
roved impossible to generate data relevant to some aspects of the alleged
lecline'. Accurate figures were not available on such matters as attendance
t Ward and General Management Committee meetings over a period of
ears – which would have been useful for the purpose of constructing, say, a

comparative index of activism in different historical periods. But all of t[
evidence presented here is highly relevant to the Hindess argument – ar
similar kinds of assertions – and the evidence is, I believe, sufficient to ca
serious doubts on – if not 'refute' – many of the kinds of argument which i
volve alleged 'decline' and 'de-radicalization'.

Turnout, Membership and Participation

The first assertion I examined in relation to the Labour Party in Kem[
town was that 'There has been, in many areas, an absolute decline in votir
and other forms of orthodox political activity'. I take this to mean a decline i
electoral turnout, especially in working class areas,[6] and a decline i
membership of, participation in, and activity concerned with orthodo
political organizations like local Labour Parties. The evidence accumulate
so far indicates that this is not the case in Brighton, Kemptown.

For the whole of the old County Borough of Brighton, turnout in the a[
nual municipal elections has remained remarkably stable at around 40 p[
cent for some fifty five years[7] (see Figure 1 and Appendix B). The annu.
average turnout in all wards over this period has been 39·93 per cent, peak
and lows generally conforming to national trends. The peaks were 45·1 p[
cent in 1920 (9 wards contested[8]), 45·8 per cent in 1931 (13 contested
46·6 per cent in 1949 (13 contested) and 48·1 per cent and 47·1 per cent i
1952 and 1953 (14 and 17 contests). Subsequent but lower peaks of 44·
per cent and 42·5 per cent occurred in 1957 and 1967 (7 and 19 contests
Below average turnouts occurred in 1921–4, 1928–30, 1932, 1937, 1945–[
1960–2, 1964, 1966 and 1968–74 inclusive.

On a decade by decade basis turnout averaged around 39 per cent in th
1920s, rose to around 40 per cent in the 1930s, rose again to around 41 pe
cent in the 1940s and to around 43 per cent in the 1950s. The annu[
average for all wards fell to around 38 per cent in the 1960s, and to date i
has been just under 37 per cent in the early 1970s. For Brighton as a whol
the graph (see Figure 1) shows that there has been a steady decline in tur
nout since the mid-fifties broken only by significant increases in 1963, 196[
and 1973. If anything, the graph shows a slight overall decline of aroun[

---

[6] See also Hindess, *op. cit.*, p. 56, and p. 163.

[7] 1918 was chosen as the starting point of this analysis because the proportion of the population wit[
the vote prior to the introduction of the new franchise was so small. In Brighton, 22,936 electors wer
on the Register in 1915; in 1918 the new Register contained the names of 83,600 electors.

[8] There were 14 wards in Brighton prior to 1928, and since 1928 there have been 19 wards.

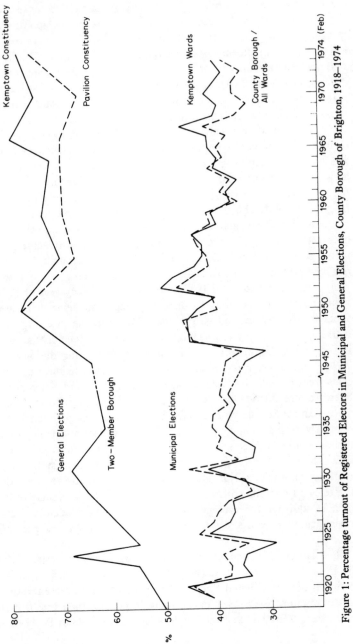

Figure 1: Percentage turnout of Registered Electors in Municipal and General Elections, County Borough of Brighton, 1918–1974

one per cent over the fifty-five year period, but in another sense one cou
say that turnout in the late sixties and early seventies appears to ha
returned to the levels of the early and late twenties, when, of course, t]
electorate was much smaller as a proportion of the population.

If we examine turnout on a constituency basis, then some interestin
differences emerge between the predominantly working class Kemptow
wards and wards in the more middle class Pavilion Constituency. T]
former area is politically marginal, and was captured by Labour in 19￼
and 1966. The latter has always been a safe Tory seat, as was the old tw￼
member Constituency comprising the whole Borough which existed pri￼
to 1950. Keen psephologists will not need reminding that the two bigge￼
majorities ever recorded in General Elections in Britain – 63,253 ar
63,041 – were achieved by the Tory/National Government candidates ￼
Brighton in 1931. The graph shows a tendency for turnout in Kemptown ￼
be increasing slowly, and the annual average for the Kemptown wards h￼
been above average for the whole Borough continuously since 1964, or
would suspect a clear indication of the effects of marginality. Turnout ￼
the Kemptown wards was below the Borough average for almost ever
year during the 1920s and 1930s. Prior to the midway year of 1948, tu￼
nouts in Kemptown averaged around 37 per cent, but since 1948 the annu￼
average has been around 42 per cent. Therefore, generalizing the mor
working class Kemptown one might be tempted to conclude that turnout ￼
in fact increasing in working class areas. Generalizing the more middl
class Pavilion we would conclude that turnout in predominantly middl
class areas is declining since average turnouts of around 43 per cent in th
twenties and thirties had fallen to around 40 per cent in the fifties an
sixties. In the last six years this decline in Pavilion Constituency has bee￼
relatively dramatic, and can be traced to an even more startling decline i￼
turnout in two or three safe Tory middle class 'suburban' Wards. In Kemp
town, there is no evidence of any major decline in turnout in the traditiona
working class wards. Nor, in so far as I have been able to ascertain fron
the relevant data, has there been any decline in Labour's share of the poll
and, in addition, the average number of Labour Councillors elected ha
risen steadily over the fifty-five year period, reaching a new peak of 28 i￼
1973.

The annual affiliated membership of Labour Party organizations i￼
Brighton has generally followed national trends. Until 1911, there is n￼
mention of any affiliated Labour Party or Labour Representation Committee organization in the official Annual Reports of the Party. But what i￼
interesting to note is that the Brighton and Hove Labour Party remaine￼

emarkably small throughout the period from 1918 to 1929. Although affiliated membership figures are not available for most of this period, the record of affiliation fees paid would suggest that total membership was less than 200 in these years (see Appendix C). Moreover, throughout the thirties, when the annual affiliated membership figures are available, the total membership of the Labour Party in Brighton and Hove never exceeded 762, if we ignore the 1938 figure which included the Trades Council. The average membership for the period – around 500 – was tiny compared with the population of the Brighton and Hove conurbation (see Figure 2). On the basis of these figures alone, it would seem unlikely that a thriving and active Labour party existed in Brighton during the interwar period, and additional scraps of information – like the records of attendance at Labour Party Women's section meetings – confirm that participation levels were not high. If there was a 'Golden Age' of local Labour party activity in Brighton, it wasn't the period prior to 1914, and it is unlikely to have been the period between the wars.

As we saw in Chapter Four, the evidence from other parts of the country seems to indicate that the post-war period from 1945 into the early 1950s represented very much a heyday for local Labour parties. This was undoubtedly so in Brighton, judging by the membership figures.[9] Membership of the Labour Party in Brighton climbed dramatically from 80 in 1944 to a peak of 3,467 in 1952. After 1952, it tumbled almost as dramatically but levelled off at a higher level of around 2,000 for most of the late 1950s and early 1960s. With the introduction of the 1,000 minimum affiliation rule for all CLPs in 1963, the total affiliated membership figure becomes distorted, since it cannot drop below 2,000. But Kemptown CLP records going back to 1957 provide a more accurate picture of the total membership of Kemptown CLP, and these have been included in the table in Appendix C, along with the 1973 figure for Pavilion CLP. In Kemptown in 1969, recorded membership fell as low as 628, yet Kemptown CLP, like most other CLPs, had to affiliate on the basis of 1,000 members. Moreover, real membership was probably even lower than recorded membership, and a check on the recorded membership of 927 for Kemptown CLP in 1973 revealed that real membership was more likely to be around 850 (see the discussion of this problem in Appendix A). The recorded membership of Pavilion CLP in 1973 was 384, indicating that real membership was more likely to be around 350.

We have, therefore, three measures of CLP membership – affiliated

---

[9] Personal reminiscences also tend to corroborate this.

recorded, and real. The first in most cases is the minimum figure of 1,000 which gives no indication of memberships lower than 1,000, but does indicate higher memberships more accurately. The second, recorded membership, refers to the CLP's own membership lists which tend to exaggerate slightly the real membership, and the real membership can only really be established by seeking out every listed member. In 1973, while the affiliated membership of the two Brighton CLPs was 2,000, the recorded membership was 1,311, and I would estimate that the real membership was around 1,200. This is well above any figure recorded in the 1920s and 1930s, and allowing for some slight exaggeration in recorded membership it was only substantially exceeded in the period 1947–1960. Real membership was slightly above the 1,200 mark between 1963 and 1967 but the average for the 1960s and 1970s has been 1,168. In fact, the only decade in which real membership consistently and substantially exceeded this figure was the 1950s, which covered some of the exceptional post-war period I earlier called the heyday of local Labour parties.

An examination of levels of activity among members in Kemptown today, reveals, as one would expect, that very few Labour Party members are remotely active in the local party. Members were asked in the survey whether they had done anything in the recent local elections, and told to indicate what they had done from a list of eight different activities. Fifty seven per cent of the 61 per cent who returned the questionnaire – maybe 74 per cent or more overall – said that they had done nothing, although nearly one half of these had put up a window-bill. Election-wise, only 13 per cent of the respondents could be considered as being 'very active', and a similar figure emerged for meeting attendance. Fifteen per cent said they had attended a party meeting in the last month. A picture therefore emerges of a core of membership – about 13–15 per cent of the respondents or about 8–9 per cent of the membership – who could be considered to be 'activists'. I shall examine their class characteristics below in relation to the middle-class takeover thesis.

Activists tend to be more left-wing than the rest of the membership. While 53 per cent of all Labour Party members in Kemptown want the Party to be 'more socialist', 87 per cent of those 'very active' in the 1973 Municipal Elections wanted the Party to be 'more socialist'. A similar pattern emerged when I looked at the views of the meeting-attenders. Seventy eight per cent of those attending meetings in the last month wanted the Party to be 'more socialist' – none said 'less' – but only 35 per cent of those who had never attended a Labour Party meeting wanted the Party to be 'more socialist'.

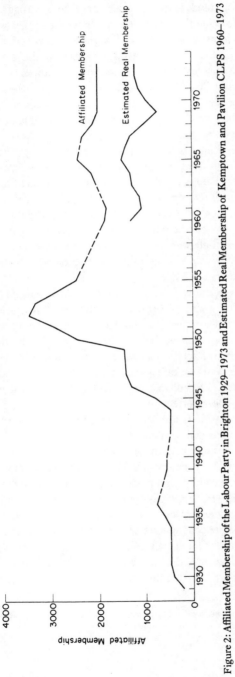

Figure 2: Affiliated Membership of the Labour Party in Brighton 1929–1973 and Estimated Real Membership of Kemptown and Pavilion CLPS 1960–1973

Activists also tend to see politics more as a struggle between 't working class versus the bosses' (or 'the haves' and 'have-nots') but th were no more or less inclined to say that there was a good deal of differen between the parties. The leadership choices of the electoral activis (60 in all) also contrasted with the leadership choices of all responden (464). 'Left-wing' leaders obtained 48 per cent of the activists' vot (against 39 per cent for 'centre' and 'right-wing' leaders), but only 21 p cent of the votes of the whole membership, who mostly (52 per cen preferred Harold Wilson to remain as leader.

Public ownership of production was also selected by the activists as th second most important area of national concern – it only rated joi seventh with the membership at large – and they rated it much higher, to when asked which ideas were closest to their idea of socialism. It was s cond only to 'creating social equality' as encapsulating their idea socialism, but among the whole membership it was only the sixth mo popular choice. In answer to the open-ended question on the meaning socialism, public ownership and the abolition of capitalism was easily th most popular activist choice.[10]

I also asked respondents when they thought that they had been most a tive in the Party, giving 8 periods from 'pre 1918' to '1971–3'. By far th largest proportion – 38 per cent – opted for the last two years. Apart fro the obvious ageing process, this may be accounted for by the fact that th Kemptown Labour Party has a considerable turnover of membership. F instance, 42 per cent had only joined in the last six years and 53 per cent i the last ten years. The collapse in 1967–9 is reflected in Kemptown in th rupture of an almost perfect continuum in activity-periods from pre-191 to the present day. It is also interesting to note that Hindess specified decline in *orthodox* political activity, linking this with the growth of le groups and community activities during the 1966–70 Labour governmen But few Labour Party members in Kemptown were obviously involved i other activities, and although most said that there were now more group and campaigns – 71 per cent against 6 per cent – fewer said that the themselves were more rather than less active in these kinds of campaign and groups – 18 per cent against 23 per cent. This tends to corroborate th earlier evidence of Gould, who found that members of 'Riverside' CL were not significantly active in other forms of voluntary associations, an he concluded that 'membership of the Labour Party, far from spurrin

---

[10] The reader is advised to consult the *New Statesman* articles for a fuller account of the replies these questions, see footnote 3 of this chapter.

them on to wider participation in community life, acts as an absorbing substitute for it'.[11] When morale is temporarily low, as it was in the period 1966–70, it is more likely that the majority of Labour Party members who drop of political activity, will tend to drop out altogether, rather than join community action or left groups.

Party and Class

The second assertion I wished to examine was that 'the close association between party and social class has itself declined and, with the progressive disappearance of the class polarization of formal politics, there has been a decline in political activity resulting from identification with, and commitment to, the interests of the working class as such'.[12]

The relationship between party and class, and the extent to which party members and activists identify with, and are committed to 'the working class as such' *today* was therefore one of the prime matters for investigation in the Kemptown study. The survey showed that Kemptown Labour Party is predominantly composed of skilled and unskilled workers, but slightly less so than either the local or national population as a whole. Of the 64 per cent of respondents who were economically active, 39·0 per cent were skilled manual workers, 20·9 per cent were unskilled manual workers, 27·6 per cent were white collar workers and 12·5 per cent were employed in professional or managerial occupations. Seventy four per cent of all members had fathers who were either unskilled or skilled manual workers, 72 per cent had only been to secondary or elementary school, 75 per cent had left school at the age of 15 years or under, and 67 per cent preferred to describe themselves as 'working class' rather than 'middle class' or 'no particular class'.

This tends to suggest that the link between party and class in the membership is as strong as ever, but evidence for the perceived class polarization of party politics was less strong. Butler and Stokes have data on this, based on a national sample of *working-class Labour* electors, which indicates that between 31 and 44 per cent see *politics* as the conflict of class interests (depending on age). Among *all* Labour Party members in Kemptown, only 36 per cent see the difference between the political *parties* in *explicitly* class terms. The majority (52 per cent) preferred descriptions

[11] Gould, J., *'Riverside', Fabian Journal*, 1954, no. 14.

[12] Hindess, *op. cit.*, p. 163.

referring to different social priorities and so on. On the other hand, whil
Butler and Stokes found that only between 29 and 38 per cent of workin
class Labour electors thought that there was a good deal of differenc
between the parties, 52 per cent of *all* members in Kemptown thought so.

Broken down by class, it is, however, the *working-class* Labou
members who see *party* politics *more* in class terms – 40 per cent for th
C2s and DEs against only 26 per cent for the ABs and CIs. And th
working-class members are also *more* likely to see a good deal of differenc
between the parties – 57 per cent for the C2s and DEs, and 39 per cent fo
the ABs and CIs. In addition, the second and third most popular *descrip
tions* of the Labour Party and the second and third most popular *features* c
the Labour Party (out of ten choices) were that it was 'the Party of th
working class' and 'the Party of Ordinary People' which compares witl
Abrams and Rose's survey ten years earlier when only 27 per cent of hi
respondents (Labour electors) said that 'the Party of the working-clas
was one of the four most important features of the party. If there *is*
'progressive disappearance' or the class polarization of formal politics, i
certainly hasn't disappeared yet among Labour Party members in Kemp
town. But has there been a decline in *activity* resulting from identificatio
with the working class?

When I asked respondents what was the *one* main reason why the
belonged to, and/or worked for the Labour Party, by far the most popula
response (out of eight choices) was to 'further the interests of the workin
class', 36 per cent said this, and 19 per cent said to 'achieve socialism', th
second most popular. It was the respondents in the working class ward
who preferred both of these choices, and one interesting finding was tha
the respondents in the working class wards which had a substantial middl
class presence were much more keen on furthering the interests of th
working class – relative deprivation might be an explanation of this.

Concern with the 'working class as such' was also evident in response t
the questions on the meaning of socialism. An earlier question had in
dicated that 53 per cent of the respondents wanted the Labour Party to b
'more socialist', 5 per cent 'less socialist' and 35 per cent 'about the same'
with 7 per cent not replying. It seemed therefore valid to ask respondent
what they meant by 'socialist', and here specifically class concerns or mor
particularly concern with class inequalities were dominant. Althoug
'raising the standard of living' obtained the single highest rating of 33 pe
cent, 'creating equality' and 'equality of opportunity' obtained together
rating of 22 per cent. Only 'world peace' with 26 per cent came as high i
these fixed-choice responses. But the class-breakdown revealed that whils

here was no great class difference in the choice of equality and equality of opportunity, the working class respondents were about equally as keen to abolish classes (12 per cent *v* 11 per cent) but were much keener to see the liberation of the working class' (15 per cent *v* 8 per cent). In the replies to the open-ended question on socialism, the two most popular choices were variations on the equality and equality of opportunity themes (11 per cent and 9 per cent), and working class respondents were marginally keener on these. Among the great range of replies to this question, it is interesting to note that the third place was taken by variations of the phrase 'raising the standard of living of the workers'. This was especially popular among working class respondents. However, if the three categories embracing variations of 'public ownership', 'the abolition of capitalism/socialist revolution' and 'Clause 4' were combined, then this one category easily registered the largest proportion of replies received, and was particularly popular with *middle class* supporters. The *working class* respondents were concerned primarily with the central issue of working class living standards, and in this they clearly 'identified with the working class as such'.

A Middle Class Takeover?

The third and perhaps most interesting assertion involves the alleged shifting class basis of the Labour Party, and the celebrated 'middle class takeover' thesis. 'Changes in the Labour Party,' says Hindess, 'and in the urban environment, have led to the differentiation of the political demands, concerns, and orientations of party workers and supporters in the different areas.'[13]

As we have seen, the argument is essentially that the Labour Party membership is becoming disproportionately middle class as the working class members are alienated by the local and national performance of the Labour Party, and because the middle class members are also disproportionately more active, the Party has become, at the local level, strongest in the middle class areas and weakest in the working class areas, a dramatic change from the 1950s when the reverse was true. The consequence of *this* process is that there is a shift of power in local Labour Parties towards the middle class areas, and hence towards middle class policy concerns and political orientations. With local policy determination largely in the hands

---

[13] Hindess, *op. cit.*, p. 164.

of those from the middle class areas, the vicious circle of decline in the
working class areas is complete.

This again is a difficult theory to test, particularly in an area such as
Kemptown, which, because of its smaller size, does not exhibit quite the
residential segregation that probably occurs in larger cities. However, it
was possible to classify the ten wards in Kemptown into two general types
– any four-fold classification would have been artificially superimposed.
There are five more or less safe Labour wards in Kemptown, which have
an above-average proportion of both C2 and DE manual workers in their
electorate. These could be described as 'respectable working class'. And
there are five wards which are generally either safely non-Labour or are
marginal wards with a non-Labour bias, which have varying but above
average proportions of AB or CI non-manual workers in their electorate.
These may be described as either 'middle class' or 'lower middle class'
wards.

Before I examine ward differentiation, I should comment on the
relationship between *activism* and class, in particular the extent to which
middle class members are disproportionately more active. I have already
shown that the membership as a whole is only slightly more middle class
than the local electorate, and the argument from the results of other and
earlier studies, and, indeed, from the history of the Labour Party, suggests
that this has always been the case. Hindess' first proposition is therefore
dubious. The Labour Party membership is not necessarily *becoming* more
middle class. It probably always has been to some extent. However, there is
some evidence for a slight drift toward upward *economic* mobility among
current members. For instance, of the economically active members, only
29 of the 37 AB members had AB fathers, and only 58 of the 81 CI members
had CI fathers. But there were 152 C2 fathers to only 114 C2 members, and
121 DE fathers to only 59 DE members.

The second proposition of the middle class takeover thesis is that middle
class members are disproportionately active. This is undoubtedly so in
Kemptown, whatever the measure used. While only 13 per cent of *all*
members were 'very active' in elections, 39 per cent of the ABs were 'very
active', as were 23 per cent of the CIs but only 11 per cent of the C2s and a
mere 7 per cent of the DEs were 'very active'. While 15 per cent of *all*
members had attended party meetings in the last month, 32 per cent of the
ABs and 31 per cent of the CIs had, but only 12 per cent of the C2s and 10
per cent of the DEs had attended a party meeting in the last month. Put
another way, the data show that the ABs only account for 8 per cent of the
membership, but 23 per cent of the electoral activists and 16 per cent of the

meeting attenders. Conversely, skilled and unskilled manual workers represent 39 per cent of the economically-active membership, but only 26 per cent of the electoral activists and 27 per cent of the meeting attenders.

Combining meeting attendance, electoral activity and past or present officership into a single *composite index* of activism, we find that 51 per cent of the ABs and 31 per cent of the CIs are 'highly' or 'very highly' active, but the same can only be said for 11 per cent of the C2s and 12 per cent of the DEs. Put another way still, the *mean activism rating* of the average AB member is 2·351, the CI member 1·827, the C2 member 1·202 and the DE member 1·237 – denoting a fairly clear relationship between class and activism. Middle class members are therefore disproportionately more active than working class members. However, activism is not related to relative upward economic mobility. Middle class members are more active whatever their father's occupation. One idea I had, based on observation, was that *the* most active were those who had achieved upward economic mobility, chiefly through higher education, but who retained working class allegiances and militancy because of their working class background. But this didn't appear to be the case. When I controlled for father's occupation, no clear relationship emerged between mobility and activism. The single most active groups that emerged were students with AB and CI fathers (rating 3·166), CIs with CI fathers (rating 2·500), and ABs with AB fathers (rating 2·462). Overall, there was a barely *positive* relationship between activism and upward mobility among ABs (2·375 *v* 2·231), whilst in the case of upwardly mobile CIs, the relationship was actually *negative* (1·549 *v* 2·322), that is, they were *less* likely to be more active.

The proposition that middle class members are more active therefore is borne out, but the next proposition, that in consequence ward organization is *strongest* in the middle class areas and *weakest* in the working class areas is more doubtful. Without commenting on the *perceived* strength of ward organization, I can answer this in relation to the membership data, and the answer is that this is *not* the case in Kemptown, nor do I think that there is much historical evidence to suggest that there have been any dramatic changes since the 1950s.

In terms of the actual number of active members as a proportion of the total membership in each ward, it is the working class wards which are more likely to have a higher than average percentage of active and very active members. The average percentage is 18·6. Two out of five working class wards are above average, but only one of the five middle class wards is above average. When the moderately-active members are included, it is the middle class wards which do slightly better than the average of 40·0 per

cent – four out of five are above average, against three out of five working
class wards.

Broken down into electoral activity and attendance at meetings, there is,
first, no difference between the wards in the percentage of members who
are very active at election times. Both types of ward register two out of five
above the average of 15 per cent. But second, it is the working class wards
which are more likely to have a higher percentage of members who regularly attend meetings – three out of five above the average of 38·5 per cent
against two out of five for the middle class wards. On the other hand, the
working class wards are more likely to have an unstable membership –
three out of five against two out of five for the middle class wards. But the
average percentage of unstable members – those who have left and rejoined
the Party once or more – is only 10·8 per cent and the range is not
dramatic.

When these measures are combined with the percentage who are past or
present officers, and collapsed into the composite index of activism, the
following picture emerges: while the mean activism rating is 3·092 for all
members in all wards, the overall rating for the five working class wards is
3·118, and for the five middle class wards it is 3·108 i.e. there is no significant difference. But whereas two out of five middle class wards are above
average, three out of five working class wards are above average. One could
conclude on this basis that the working class wards are slightly more likely
to have an active membership.

Broken down further into two *other* ward classifications – one electoral,
the other based on socio-economic groups, we find that the safe Labour
wards register a mean activism rating of 3·118, and the safely non-Labour
wards rate much lower at 2·555, but the highest rating of 3·480 is achieved
by the marginal wards with a non-Labour bias. Clearly marginality is important here, but the safe Labour wards are in fact stronger than the safely
non-Labour wards. However, the second three-fold classification on the
basis of S.E.G.s indicates that the reverse is true. Here the clearly middle
class wards register an activism rating of 3·622, the clearly working class
wards register an activism rating of 3·118 again, with the lower middle
class/skilled working class wards registering only 2·766.

The evidence therefore is inconclusive, but the fact that (a) the safe
Labour wards register higher on the activism scale than the safely non-
Labour wards, and (b) that the overall rating indicates that the working
class wards are slightly more active, are sufficient to cast doubt on the third
proposition in the Hindess argument. There is *no* evidence in Kemptown
that the disproportionate activism of middle class Party members is part of

an *overall* and inevitable *process* which leads to the middle class wards being strongest and the working class wards being weakest, though specific instances could be quoted. Overall, the opposite tends to be the case.

Given that the third proposition falls, then one would expect its alleged consequence and the fourth proposition – that there is an accompanying shift of power in local Labour Parties toward the middle class areas – would also fall. And although I had no data on such matters as the weight carried by Councillors and committee-members from the wards in the middle class areas, personal observation of policy-determination at GMC and EC meetings of the party, and at Council meetings, would suggest that the wards in the middle class areas are by no means in control of the Party. There has been no overall obvious shift in power towards the middle class areas. In consequence, there cannot be a shift toward 'middle class policy concerns and orientations' in this way (although, and this is important, there is evidence that this may be occurring at the Council level through other mechanisms, chiefly the activists of middle class pressure-groups outside the Labour Party). But there is no clear evidence of 'differentiation of political demands, concerns and orientations among party workers and supporters in the different areas'.

Hindess argues that the ward parties in the working class areas are almost solely concerned with housing and corporation activity, whilst the Ward parties in the middle class areas are interested mostly in immigration, foreign policy, traffic control and education. He further implies that the former are more left-wing and traditionally socialist, and the latter are right-wing and technocratic. When I examined the concerns and orientations of the members in the different types of ward in Kemptown, no such overall pattern emerged:

First, I looked at the reasons why members in the different types of ward belong to the Labour Party. Here there was a slight tendency for the members in the working class wards to be more likely to say that the one main reason they belong to the Labour Party was to 'further the interests of the working class'. Against an average of 36 per cent for all wards, this was said by 38 per cent in the working class wards, but only 32 per cent in the middle class wards. Members in the working class wards were also slightly more likely to see the Labour Party as 'the Party of the working class', and members in the working class wards were slightly more likely to give further the interests of the working class' as their one main reason for joining the Party.

Second, members in the working class wards were keener on the Labour Party being 'more socialist' – three out of five were above average, but the difference was not significant.

Third, in relation to the meaning of socialism, as measured in the fixed-choice question, members in the working class wards were apparently less keen on abolishing classes, no different in their keenness to liberate the working class, more keen to raise their standard of living, more keen on public ownership, no different in their desire to see equality, and less keen on creating equality of opportunity and real democracy – altogether a pretty inconclusive picture, though the slight 'left-wing' bias detectable in the first two measures is still visible as far as the working class wards are concerned. It is not so obvious in the answers to the open-ended question of socialism because here the simple and central concern of members in the working class wards was with raising working class living standards.

In a separate, general, four-fold classification of these replies into materialistic/idealistic, specific/general, sectarian/non-sectarian and micro or macro conceptions of socialism, a more interesting situation occurred: members in the working class wards got a materialist rating of plus 64 against a rating of minus 50 for middle class wards, a specific v general issues rating of minus 29 against minus 28, a sectarian rating of minus 108 against minus 149, and a micro v. macro rating of minus 121 against minus 67. In other words, the conceptions of socialism among members in the working class wards in relation to those in the middle class wards are that they are much more materialistic, they are no more and no less keen on general principles rather than specific issues, they are more sectarian in their emphasis on 'the working class', and they are more likely to adopt a total or 'holistic' approach to society. Thus on three out of four counts, Hindess would seem to be correct, at least in relation to *this* aspect of the alleged differentiation of political orientations.

Fourth, in response to the question 'Why are there different political parties', there was also a slight tendency for members in the working class wards to see politics more in terms of class conflict. Four out of five working class wards were above the average of 36 per cent with a rating of 40 per cent, whereas only three out of five middle class wards were above average, but the difference is not significant.

Fifth, members in the working class wards were slightly less likely to see a 'good deal of difference' between the parties. Only one out of the five working class wards was above the average of 52 per cent, whereas two out of five of the middle class wards were above the average. If Hindess is saying that the working class are more alienated from party politics, then this would tend very slightly to support his case. But in relation to the importance attached to different policy concerns – and here I only have data on national issues – the Hindess argument is not supported: housing, for instance, is the overwhelmingly dominant policy concern of members in both working class and middle class wards, indeed more so in the latter. Education is only slightly more dominant a concern in the middle class wards, but immigration, foreign policy and defence are more important in the working class wards, not the middle class – precisely the opposite of what Hindess apparently found in Liverpool. Therefore, on the fourth proposition of the Hindess 'middle class take-over' thesis, the case is not proven. There is no overall evidence in Kemptown that the alleged process of differentiation of policy concerns and orientations is occurring.

In concluding this examination of the four basic propositions in the 'middle class take-over' thesis, the first – that the membership is disproportionately middle class – is true to some extent, but it probably always has been. The second – that the middle class members are disproportionately active – is certainly true, but again this has probably always been the case, and it is unlikely that any dramatic changes have occurred. The third – that in consequence ward organizations are strongest in the middle class areas and weakest in the working class areas – is not supported by the evidence available. And the fourth proposition – that a shift in power, policy concerns and orientations towards the middle class members has occurred – is also not supported in Kemptown. The 'middle class take-over' thesis as a whole – as described by Hindess – does not therefore seem to apply to the Labour Party in Kemptown.

Comments

This book has been a general exploration of some problems associated with the British Labour Party and its relationship with the British working class. Its aim has been to serve as an introduction to the Labour Party for all those interested in the Labour Party, and for those who see it as a problem-area. As such, it has largely consisted of a general review of some relevant literature and an appraisal of some relevant empirical evidence. By its very nature, therefore, one would expect to find a 'conclusion' to a general exploration which doesn't lead to one particular conclusion, but instead contains a series of observations.

Yet, if this book has any theme at all, it is that the Labour Party has always had an essentially passive relationship to the working class, and this is intimately related to the electoral origins and function of the Labour Party. Knowledge of the actual practice of Constituency Labour Parties reinforces this view. However, it is often implied that this is something new, and that in a number of different ways the Labour Party and 'working class politics' are on the decline. In this book, I have attempted to show that many of these theories and assertions are incorrect, that in some senses Labour's relationship to the working class has not changed that much, and that the underlying assumption of most of the 'decline' arguments — that there was some kind of 'Golden Age' of working class or Labour politics — is probably a myth. Indeed, one could argue that there are very good reasons for saying that if there is a Golden Age, it is today.

I would, however, like to correct a possibly mistaken impression I may have given, implying that there has been *no* change, that there are *no* senses in which we can speak of a 'decline' in working class or Labour politics. For instance, at the level of party rhetoric, terms like 'working class' and 'ruling class' probably do not occur quite so frequently as they did, either in party publications or in the speeches of some Labour leaders. Harold Wilson, for example, does not talk or write about 'socialism' or the 'Socialist Alter-

124

native' as frequently as, say, Clement Attlee did, or make speeches about the 'Social Revolution' in the way that even Herbert Morrison did. But this is not to say that their actions or ideas were really any different – or any more 'socialist' – or that such terms cannot be used as 'camouflage' to hide the fact that they were actually doing something entirely different. Such terms are also subject to the vagaries of fashion.

In another sense, too, we may be able to speak of a decline in Labour Party political education. Pamphlets designed to 'make converts' like 'Vote Labour? Why?' (1945) – a propagandistic work on the 'socialist message' which contained a final exhortation to 'Hand this book on to your friend who "still has his doubts"' – would seem almost inconceivable today. But it is extremely doubtful that Labour's political education effort *as a whole* is really any less significant today than it was in earlier historical periods. In these kinds of senses, senses which involve the quality and flavour of working class politics, the evidence for and against 'decline' remains essentially impressionistic or intuitive, and until more research is done or new techniques of evaluation are developed we will not be in a position to come to definitive conclusions.[1]

In the case of some other senses of 'decline' – involving such things as participation rates, membership levels and voting behaviour – we do have available data of a more objective nature from many different sources, and where possible, these have been incorporated into the test.[2] But – in short – there remain enormous problems of evaluating generalized theories of 'decline' and 'de-radicalization' and the case is by no means closed. However, the evidence outlined in this book concerning most aspects of most arguments involving 'decline' would suggest that they are usually either exaggerated or mistaken.

From the socialist point of view, they are also reactionary because their obvious corollary is that the prospects for the Labour Party and the prospects for socialism are worse today than they have ever been. But is this really so? The Labour Party, despite relatively low total polls at recent General Election, has now fully established itself as a natural governing

---

[1] John Clayton Thomas provides a valuable and unique international survey in 'The Decline of Ideology in Western Political Parties', *Sage Professional Papers in Comparative Political Sociology*, vol. 1, no. 12 (1975). Labour parties, he finds, have not moved significantly rightward.

[2] It is interesting to note that the second (1974) edition of Butler and Stokes' *Political Change in Britain* (published as I was completing this book) now has a chapter on 'The Decline of the Class Alignment'. However, the evidence on which that was based is now some years old, the 'decline' was only measured over a relatively short period, and the method of classifying respondents may have ignored a 'hidden' working class, often mistakenly classified as 'middle class' – see Colin S. Rallings in the *British Journal of Political Science*, vol. 5, no. 1, p. 107.

party. On balance, demographic trends are likely to work in Labour's electoral favour for the next couple of decades.[3] Politically, the Labour Party's current programme is indeed (superficially) more radical than any other policy document adopted since 1945. There are more general reasons, too, which suggest that the prospects for socialism in Britain have never been better. Relevant considerations would be the continued erosion of working class deference, the diminished role of religious ideology, the existence of wider educational opportunities, and the probable existence of a new generation of radical 'post-materialists' – apart from the rapidly changing international balance of forces and a rapidly developing economic situation which will increasingly demand new kinds of measures, especially new kinds of state intervention in the economy. Most important of all, the backbone of the Labour Party – the Trade Union movement – is arguably stronger in all sorts of ways than at any time in its history.[4]

The danger of the 'Golden Age' myths is that an idealized, romanticized vision of the past facilitates on the one hand a frequent exaggeration of the actual power and influence of the Labour movement in earlier historical periods; and this at the same time leads to the common underestimation of the power of Labour under capitalism, as well as a chronic lack of confidence in the potential of the Labour movement as a force for social – and socialist – change. The 'Golden Age' myths and the theories of 'decline' and 'deradicalization' should be demolished on these grounds alone.

---

[3] See Butler and Stokes, *op. cit.*, 2nd edition.
[4] See Barratt-Brown, M., *From Labourism to Socialism*, Spokesman, 1972.

Appendices

Appendix A

The 1973 Kemptown Survey

Administration

Having resolved to get as much relevant information as possible about the present views and characteristics of Labour Party members in Kemptown, I was faced with the problem of how to get it, and how to get it relatively quickly and cheaply. The use of the survey questionnaire technique proved essential in this case, particularly for the acquisition of data on the basic characteristics of the membership.

Once the decision to administer a questionnaire had been taken, I first had to choose between the obvious alternatives, a mailed self-completion exercise for all 900 members or personal interviews with a quota or random sample. I rejected both, the first because I obviously wanted a high response rate, the second because I wanted to 'get to' every member. By rejecting the second, I could also mostly eliminate sampling-error and interviewer-bias (the pilot interviews I had conducted indicated that interviewer-bias was likely to be extreme in this kind of survey). Because official membership lists are reputed to be inaccurate, I wanted a *complete* survey as a check on the lists, but I also wanted the questionnaire to be self-completion exercise. In any case, to interview all 900 members would have either taken about a year or would have cost a great deal of money which I didn't have.

The following solution evolved: I would design a simple but thorough questionnaire suitable for self-completion, and personally deliver it with a covering letter in order to boost-up the response rate. I would leave the respondents to complete it in private in their own time and return it anonymously in a pre-paid envelope. The initial contact would be followed-up by a mailed reminder. After a trial-run in one ward, I realized that this technique was feasible and adequate, although the response rate in this ward (over 70 per cent) was not quite matched in all other wards. That this technique did prove feasible in practice may be attributed in part to my personal role, in part to the *content* of the questionnaire and in part to the *form* in which it was presented.

First, I had been active in the local party for sometime prior to the administration of the questionnaire, and I knew personally a fair number of members particularly in the wards adjacent to my home. Moreover, key members of the party knew that I was carrying-out some kind of 'study' for some time before, so the ground was reasonably well prepared. Most important of all, I was able to introduce myself to respondents on their doorsteps as being a member 'from Queens Park Ward Labour Party'.

Second, there is no doubt in my mind that the actual content of the questionnaire proved stimulating and attractive, which is precisely what it was intended to be. Some respondents actually enjoyed filling it in, indeed, one or two wrote to me or added notes on the bottom of the questionnaire saying just that. The chance to 'vote' on the most important issues of the day or for one of the 'candidates' for the party leadership gave the survey a participatory flavour. The chance to say what one really thought about the Labour Party or politicians in general had the same effect. The main point here for the researcher is, of course, that if you go to politically-concerned people personally and ask them for *their* views, and what they really think about such and such, they feel to some extent flattered, and they will respond. This is especially so when the respondents are members of a political party who inevitably feel that their views are neglected by their leaders in the House of Commons. The only contact most members have with their party is when somebody occasionally calls asking for money. Rarely are they asked for their opinions.

Third, this technique was also made feasible by the form of the questionnaire. It was presented as a *complete* survey of every Labour Party member in Kemptown, a kind of 'opinion poll' of the membership, which it was. The need for a high response-rate was pointed out in the covering letter, and the questionnaire was clearly anonymous.

The sample used in this survey consisted, therefore, of every member of the Kemptown Constituency Labour Party. Since nobody can say with great precision exactly who are the individual members of the Labour Party in Kemptown at any given time, I had to use as my source of information that which I and the Secretary-Agent deemed most accurate. These were the 'street-sheets' of members submitted from, or cajoled out of the ward secretaries by the Secretary-Agent, and these constituted my operational definition of 'member'. They list every member in each individual street together with a record of their subscription payments. For six wards only the 1972 lists were available, but four wards had submitted their 1973 lists by this time (July 1973).

Official party membership lists are reputed to be inaccurate, and my subsequent experiences suggested that this is the case but only to some extent. But because the greatest proportion of respondents 'lost' were those who had moved, the only major criticism that could be made of these street-sheets was that they were somewhat out-of-date. In the case of one ward, there was evidence to suggest that the street-sheets were incomplete and perhaps twenty members had been missed, but by and large they tended to slightly overestimate the membership – they included, for instance, members who had moved or who had stopped paying subs for a year or more. In addition, the 1972 street-sheets for six wards did not include any *new* members who might have joined in the preceding year, though my estimate was that they were very few in number. Certainly, I knew of no membership drives in this period, primarily because most ward Parties were fully occupied in preparing for the two rounds of local elections in June and April 1973.

Bearing in mind that the very concept of 'membership of the party' is a tricky one, I had to base the survey on some defined population such as 'members', and this would of course include the categories of 'activist', 'Officer' and 'Councillor'. The Secretary-Agent's lists were clearly the most reliable source of membership information.

Distribution of the questionnaire took place between July 19th and August 31st 1973, taking just over six weeks in all. As a substantial proportion of the membership consisted of husbands and wives and sometimes whole families, the number of separate calls required totalled less than six hundred. Averaging about twenty calls in an evening, I managed to deliver all the questionnaire kits in thirty days.[1] Weekend delivery proved impractical in view of the high number of respondents who were out or busy, and I found that the best time for calling was between about 6.30 p.m. and 9.00 p.m. on weekday evenings. A very high proportion of respondents were in the house at this time, except perhaps on Fridays.

Since a high proportion of the respondents were working men or women or busy housewives, I soon learned to arrive no earlier than 6.30 p.m. so as

---

[1] The 'kit' included a personally-addressed envelope, covering letter, the questionnaire itself and a pre-paid addressed envelope.

not to clash with their arrival home from work or the evening meal. People also tend to be more receptive after dinner. I found it fatal to arrive during the six o'clock news bulletin and it proved impossible to 'chat-up' respondents about the importance and purposes of the questionnaire if my arrival at the doorstep coincided with a popular TV programme. Often my introductory remarks were far too brief. In fact, as soon as I heard the theme tune of 'Coronation Street' come wafting out of the windows on these summer evenings, I used to pack up and go off for a pint.

Sometimes I felt like a salesman with one foot in the door, but on other occasions I was warmly welcomed and invited in to explain the survey more fully or talk about the Tory Government, the state of the Labour Party, or the performance of a local Councillor. Brief though most of them were, I learned much from these conversations.

Where the member did not come to the door but was in the house, I explained that it was about the Labour Party, and asked to see the member personally. Invariably, he or she came to the door with money in hand or saying something like 'I suppose you want some money', assuming that I was a sub-collector. Where the household contained two or more members, I asked to see them all personally. Where one or more members were out, but at least one was in, I generally explained the survey to the member present and asked them to explain it in turn to the other or other members of the household. On the whole people were very keen to do this, and many offered to do it before I had an opportunity to ask. If no member was in and somebody else answered the door, I generally said that I would call back, although this did not always happen mainly because the son/daughter/husband/wife/grandparent/lodger would insist that they give it to the member or members concerned, to save me a journey. Where nobody was in, I called back, and continued to call back, often leaving a gap of two weeks in case the member or members concerned were on holiday (but remarkably few seemed to be at this peak in the holiday season). After three separate negative visits, I marked the respondent down as a non-contact. In all, twenty-eight of the original list of 927 members fell into this category, and a record of all contacts in each ward appears below (Table 1).

What I actually said to the potential respondents was largely conditioned by my immediate impression of them and the manner in which they responded to my initial introduction. I generally played it by ear, but I usually made a number of key points including: the fact that it was a complete survey of every member of the Labour Party in Kemptown Constituency; that it was designed to find out something about who is the Labour Party these days; that it was a kind of 'opinion poll', providing each

Table 1

Contact Sheet

	Listed members	Resident Councillors	Moved	Wrong Address or Untraceable	Self-assigned 'non Member' or 'left'	Non-contact after three visits	Dead or in Hospital	Elderly: Questionnaire completion impossible	Questionnaire refused or returned incomplete	Maximum possible replies
Queen's Park '73	79	–	5	–	–	1	1	–	3	69
Hanover '72	65	1	10	–	1	–	2	–	–	51
Elm Grove '72	107	3	7	–	–	5	4	–	–	88
King's Cliff '72	178	1	15	3	7	3	3	–	–	146
Warren '73	117	3	5	1	–	4	–	–	1	103
Pier '72	54	–	11	1	1	–	1	–	2	38
Rottingdean '72	20	–	5	–	–	–	–	–	1	14
Falmer '73	76	3	3	3	2	4	–	–	–	61
Moulescoomb '73	74	2	2	–	–	4	–	2	2	62
Lewes Road '72	148	–	7	6	5	7	1	7	3	112
Councillors '73	22	–	–	–	–	–	–	–	–	22
	940	(13)	70	14	16	28	12	9	12	766

member with the opportunity to say what they thought were the most important political issues, and what they thought of the Labour Party; that I wanted members to say exactly what they really thought; that to be representative a high response was required so that everybody's views were taken into account; that it had been approved by the officers of the Kemptown Labour Party; that it was completely anonymous and confidential; that it was very easy to complete, being largely a question of putting ticks and crosses in the appropriate boxes.

I should also say a word or two about the overall *approach* I adopted in the administration of the questionnaire. I was at great pains to present it as a 'quasi-official' and yet 'quasi-independent' enquiry. If it was seen as being an *official* 'probe' into the private lives, income, views and activity-levels of each member, then one would assume that respondents would be somewhat wary of completing it all, or would suitably modify their answers. Fears that the questionnaire was a political 'witch-hunt' or an attempt to find out who were the 'lazy members' could be easily aroused, so I had to make it clear that I was not interested in individuals, just percentages.

On the other hand I had to give the survey some legitimacy by making it 'quasi-official'. Co-operation was secured from the local party officers, and the Secretary-Agent in particular was most helpful. The Executive Committee and the General Management Committee of the Kemptown Constituency Labour Party were approached, and, despite some initial opposition, they gave their permission to let the survey go ahead. Without such permission, the survey would clearly have been impossible.

Apart from taking care to adopt the correct approach, I also had to take measures to mobilize *support* for the idea of the survey in other ways. One method was to send a letter, and subsequently talk to key activists in each Ward in an effort to convince them of the value of the questionnaire. I endeavoured to get them to do what they could in their immediate neighbourhood by way of persuading other members to participate in the survey. Another method was to attempt to stimulate discussion about the questionnaire at every level, so that the survey was given some status and importance. Finally, I persuaded the local evening paper and the local BBC radio station to give the survey coverage.

All these moves were indirect attempts to boost the response-rate. I now turn to a discussion of this.

Response Rate

The overall response-rate for the survey was 61 per cent of all possible replies (see Table 2). This rate varied between Wards from 41 per cent to 77 per cent (Table 3). I had been aiming for 70 per cent or more, and a preliminary trial-run of the 'personally-delivered self-completion technique' in my own Ward had indicated that this might be possible. However, a response-rate of 61 per cent for this kind of survey is good. I also consider it to be reasonably valid for the following reasons: The sample consisted of every 'member' of Kemptown Labour Party according to the 1972 or 1973 Ward membership lists, a total of 927 members. As Figure 2 shows, no less than 161 of these had to be eliminated from the sample because they had moved, died, etc. Of the remaining 766, it was clear, from my experiences when delivering the questionnaire, that a substantial proportion of these could not really be considered 'members' in any real sense at all.

As I point out above, many respondents were puzzled when I informed them that they were listed as members of the Labour Party, some denying it outright, saying that they were only Labour supporters or voters. Others had been signed-up by another member of the family without being aware of it.

Table 2
Response-Rate

Total listed membership	918
plus 9 non-resident Councillors	927
plus 13 resident Councillors	940
Total moved	70
Total wrong-address or untraceable	14
Total self-ascribed 'non-member'	16
Total non-contacts (after 3 visits)	28
Total dead or in hospital	12
Total elderly: completion impossible	9
Total refusals	12
Maximum possible replies	940 minus 174
	766
Total replies received	464
Overall response rate	61%

NB. If the refusals, the elderly, the hospitalized and a proportion of the non-contacts are included as 'members', then the response-rate falls to around 59%.

Others had joined purely and simply to partake of the attractions offered by the Labour Club, and still others, particularly in one ward, had clearly been pressurized into joining by an aggressive recruiting drive in 1971–2. Only the 1972 list was available for this ward at the time of the survey, but confirmation of my suspicions came in January 1974 when the 1973 list was made available. It showed a 'loss' in one year of no less than 47 listed members in this one ward.

My argument, therefore, is that with such a large proportion of the 'membership' consisting of people who had either not *themselves* voluntarily 'joined' the Labour Party, or people who had joined but had no strong political allegiance to the Labour Party, a response-rate of 61 per cent is perhaps the most one could hope to achieve in such a situation.

In short, I would argue that a substantial proportion of the 39 per cent who were non-respondents, were also, in effect, 'non-members'. Furthermore in *any* survey there is bound to be a certain residual percentage who will never respond to any kind of questionnaire. Even poll firm interviewers regularly obtain a refusal-rate of 15–20 per cent.

Nevertheless, it would be entirely incorrect to totally *ignore* the non respondents. The very fact that 39 per cent of listed Labour Party member did not return a questionnaire about the Labour Party is significant. But in order to demonstrate that the non-response of these 39 per cent did no affect the survey findings, one would have to show that the characteristic of the non-respondents did not differ from those of the respondents.

Table 3

Response Rate by Ward

Ward	Simple Dichotomic Classification	Listed members	Maximum Possible Replies	Replies	% Reponse
Elm Grove	'Working class'	107	88	57	65%
Falmer	'Working class'	76	61	25	41%
Hanover	'Working class'	65	51	38	75%
Kings Cliff	'Middle class'	178	146	80	55%
Lewes Road	'Working class'	148	112	58	52%
Moulscoomb	'Working class'	74	62	47	76%
Pier	'Middle class'	54	38	22	58%
Queens Park	'Middle class'	79	69	53	77%
Rottingdean	'Middle class'	20	14	10	71%
Warren	'Middle class'	117	103	61	59%
Councillors		22	22	13	59%
Totals		940	766	464	61%

I have already argued that the degree of allegiance of the non respondents to the Labour Party, and hence their activity levels, are likel to be a lot lower than that of the respondents. I have taken this into accoun in my analysis of participation in the Party. I also endeavoured to ascertai the demographic characteristics of the non-respondents.

A seemingly reasonable assumption I made prior to the survey was tha the non-respondents would be more likely to be older rather than younge and more working-class than middle-class. It could, for instance, b suggested that older people would be somewhat unfamiliar with surve questionnaires. There was some evidence for this, indeed one or two older members had clearly never seen a questionnaire, nor knew what they were for. On the other hand, it was my impression that older people were more conscientious about filling it in, they seemed to attach more importance to the survey, and, of course, pensioners had more time on their hands in which to complete it. Younger members appeared to be pressed for time, especially young-marrieds with children, often saying that they might 'fill it in over the weekend', whereas pensioners tended to set about completing it right away. So the arguments from experience tend to balance the initial assumption.

Similarly, it might be thought that working class people would be less likely than middle class people to complete the questionnaire, due to their lack of education and unfamiliarity with such techniques. Here again, while there was some evidence for this, it was also the case that some middle class respondents were more blasé about the survey, and less satisfied with some of the questions – particularly abour income. I also got the distinct impression that some middle class people would, when presented with the questionnaire, say something like 'Oh super! I'll fill it in this evening', and didn't, while working class respondents tended to say 'OK mate, I'll have a go at it on Sunday afternoon' and did.

But these were only impressions. In order to obtain more objective data, a complete re-call survey would have been required. Because the questionnaire was anonymous, tracing and identifying *all* the non-respondents would have been ethically problematic, and, administratively, a mammoth task. Even then, there would be no guarantee of accuracy. It was possible, however, to examine the characteristics of the non-respondents in one Ward, where they numbered 16 out of the 69 maximum possible replies.

No definite conclusions should be made on the basis of data from one Ward alone – and one where a high overall response rate was achieved – but the results would seem to support my argument that the characteristics of the non-respondents did not, on the whole, differ very greatly from the characteristics of the respondents (see Table 4 over page).

In terms of S.E.G.s, there was a tendency for both ABs and DEs to be less likely to have returned the questionnaire, and hence be underrepresented in the sample. The extent of this is particularly marked in the case of the DEs. But because both CIs and C2s were more likely to have responded, there is no obvious difference in the overall class characteristics of the respondents and non-respondents.

The key manual/non-manual division comes between C1 and C2. Above this line are 45 per cent of the respondents and 44 per cent of the non-

Table 4

Characteristics of Respondents and Non-Respondents in Queens Park
Ward

	Socio-Economic Groups			Age	
	Respondents	Non-Respondents		Respondents	Non-Respondents
ABs	20%	31%	16–24	6%	0%
C1s	25%	13%	25–30	27%	25%
C2s	25%	13%	31–40	29%	19%
DEs	10%	25%	41–46	6%	25%
Housewives	2%	—	47–52	10%	19%
OAPs	10%	13%	53–63	8%	6%
Students	6%	6%	64–73	6%	6%
			73+	6%	0%

respondents, and below this line (the C2s and DEs) are 35 per cent of the
respondents and 38 per cent of the non-respondents in Queens Park Ward.
There would appear to be a very slight tendency, therefore, for the manual
working class as a whole to be under-represented in the sample, as is the
case with the OAPs. But if it were assumed that the non-respondents did
respond, then the proportion of members in each different S.E.G. is as
follows:

	ABs	C1s	C2s	DEs	OAPs	Students
Actual sample	20%	25%	25%	10%	10%	6%
	45%		35%			
Total membership	23%	22%	22%	14%	11%	6%
	45%		36%			

As regards age, younger people up to 40 years of age were slightly over-
represented in the sample, and older people between 41 and 52 years of age
were under-represented, as the following table shows. For members and
respondents between 53 and 73 years of age there was no difference. On the
whole, the most significant finding is that the 41–52 year olds were less
likely to have returned the questionnaire – at least in Queens Park Ward.
But the numbers involved, are, as I have already said, not very large.

	16–24	25–30	31–40	41–46	47–52	53–63	64–73	73+
Actual sample	6%	27%	29%	6%	10%	8%	6%	6%
		62%		16%				
Total membership	5%	27%	27%	11%	12%	8%	6%	5%
		59%		23%				

One final point in relation to the overall response-rate of 61 per cent: in August 1973, as I was in the process of completing my survey, *Labour Weekly* sent a simple mailed questionnaire to every Labour Party member in Kemptown. The questionnaire was preceded by a personally-signed letter from Tony Benn, and accompanied by a signed letter from the Chairman of the Constituency Party. It achieved a miserable response rate of 16 per cent which the man from Transport House described as 'very good'. In Southend it had apparently been 7 per cent.

Questionnaire Design

The research design had essentially a two-fold purpose. First, to provide a sociological portrait of a constituency Labour Party by garnering as much information as possible about the make-up and workings of the party over a period of time. Second, to test out some propositions about the alleged changing nature of local Labour politics. More specifically, this involved the accumulation and analysis of data relevant to certain propositions made by Barry Hindess in *The Decline of Working Class Politics*.

The questionnaire design reflected these concerns, and most of the questions asked in the four sections of the questionnaire were generated with these concerns specifically in mind. Because some of the Hindess propositions are of a high order of generality, and some are not amenable to 'testing' through a survey of CLP members, I cannot of course claim that the questionnaire represents a definite 'test' of the Hindess thesis.

Sections A and C contained questions designed to elicit some basic information about Labour Party members to be used mostly as independent variables in the later analysis. Section C contained highly personal but absolutely essential questions about age, income, education and parental background which might cause offence, so it was deemed politic not to place these at the beginning of the questionnaire, where they might have had a disastrous effect on the response-rate. Section A began with questions of an introductory nature. The aim of Section B was to generate some basic data on the political views of the respondents utilizing a simple opinion poll format, and Section D was an attempt to measure the influence, relevance and levels of participation in other forms of political activity on the part of Labour Party members.

The actual *format* of the questionnaire was fairly simple and straightforward in the knowledge that it was to be a self-completion exercise. The mostly multiple-choice answers were boxed-in with a space for the appropriate ticks and crosses. As is usual, this was done for ease of completion and to simplify the coding process.

As regards *style*, care was taken to hit upon a concise, but accurate wording for each question, and attempts were made to develop phrases which were as objective and unambiguous as possible. Although I did not succeed in every case, most questions were the result of a number of different drafts. Advice was sought from other researchers and pilot interviews were carried out before I arrived at the final wording for each question. No question or questionnaire is perfect, and most are a compromise with the researcher's constraints, in this case the need to gain much varied information in the space of a relatively short self-completion questionnaire. There follows a detailed description of each question.

Section A

The 'membership' problem cannot easily be resolved, so I decided to merely ask the respondents (i.e. listed 'members') whether they regarded themselves to be currently members of the Labour Party (Question 1). This provided a second check on the validity of the Secretary-Agent's lists, the first being the initial personal contact. It also served as a useful introduction to the questionnaire which made it clear to the respondents that the survey was directed at Labour Party members.

Question 2 was included to find out why listed members were no longer members, i.e. whether they had left for technical or political reasons. Even so, a problem still remained because listed members were not always aware that they were members. For instance, some respondents I encountered were not aware that the monthly payment of subs to 'the man who calls from the Labour Party' meant that they were bona-fide Labour Party members. Apart from those who described themselves on the doorstep as non-members, in practice another 4 per cent of the respondents said that they were no longer members. In order to minimize memory difficulties, a three-fold forced-response answer ('sometime this year', 'last year', 'before ast year') was offered. This would also provide a check on the state of the party organization which could be examined on a ward basis.

The aim of Question 3 was simply to find out when current members had actually joined the party. This would be of great assistance in analysing stability or instability and turnover among the membership, by comparing the characteristics of different cohorts using the same historical periods as Butler and Stokes, and interesting periods in the recent history of the Labour Party. Memory and inherent problems of the concept of membership are the main difficulties here, which only in-depth interviews could help to resolve.

Questions 4 and 5 were an attempt to locate the unstable element in the membership, primarily in order to find out their characteristics. Suggestions have been made that certain sections of the Labour Party membership may be inherently unstable. It has also been suggested that the withdrawal of different strata (e.g. middle class or working class supporters) in the membership led to the Labour collapse in 1949–51 and more particularly 1966–70. Once again, 'leaving' the party may mean either a definite political decision or a technical oversight, but the question 'Have you ever *left* and rejoined the party?' is reasonably unambiguous, as is the question 'how many times have you done this?'.

Question 6 was pretty straightforward, the object being to provide subsidiary evidence on the participation levels of members in different historical periods. The dates provided in the multiple-choice answer correspond once again to the Butler and Stokes cohorts and key dates in recent Labour Party history. It would also be possible to correlate the replies with other indeces such as age and class.

I designed Questions 7, 9 and 10 as key measures of activism, and in fact they were very successful. The categories used in the multiple-choice answers subsequently produced a valuable set of figures and as activism was to be one of the key variables in the later analysis, it was all the more pleasing that these questions 'worked'.

Activism was measured in two ways – by attendance at party meetings and by different kinds of participation in electoral activity. Observation of the operation of Kemptown CLP had suggested that these were the two main modes of participation, and therefore 'activists' could be best located by obtaining data on these topics.

I prefaced Question 7 by asking respondents whether they had *ever* attended a Labour Party meeting of any kind in an attempt to eliminate exaggeration, given that the questionnaire was quasi-official. The categories were comprehensive, ranging from 'in the last month' to 'never'

PRIVATE AND CONFIDENTIAL

QUESTIONNAIRE ON THE LABOUR PARTY

Please answer all questions as accurately and honestly as possible, and write your answers in the space provided. A cross in the appropriate box is usually all that is required.

SECTION A

1. Are you currently a member of the Labour Party? YES ☐ NO ☐

2. If you are NOT currently a member

   a) when did you decide to leave the Party?

Sometime this year	
Last year	
Before last year	

   OR b) when did you last pay a subscription?

Sometime this year	
Last year	
Before last year	

3. If you are at present a member of the Labour Party, when did you join?
   Please put a cross in the appropriate box.

Pre 1918		1931–1944		1952–1961		1967–1970	
1918–1930		1945–1951		1962–1966		1971–1973	

4. Have you ever actually left and rejoined the Party? YES ☐ NO ☐

5. If the answer is YES, how many times have you done this?
   Once ☐ Twice ☐ Three times or more ☐

6. On the whole, during which of the following periods would you say you have been most active in the Party?

Pre 1918		1931–1944		1952–1961		1967–1970	
1918–1930		1945–1951		1962–1966		1971–1973	

7. Have you ever attended a Labour Party meeting of any kind?
   If so, when did you last attend a Labour Party meeting. Was it . .

In the last month		A year ago		Twenty-five years ago	
Three months ago		Three years ago		Never	
Six months ago		Ten years ago			

8. Have you ever been an Officer of the Labour Party of any kind? YES ☐ NO ☐

9. Did you do anything in the recent local election campaigns apart from vote? YES ☐ NO ☐

10. If the answer to question 9 is YES, what exactly did you do?

Address envelopes/poll cards		Knock-up/drive a car		Man a committee room	
Deliver literature		Attend special meetings		Put up window bill	
Canvass		Telling at the poll			

11. On the whole, which is the one main reason why you belong to, and/or work for the Labour Party? Please cross one only. It is to . .

Help the Nation as a whole		Achieve social reforms	
Further the interests of the working class		Have something to do	
Keep the Tories out of power		Achieve Socialism	
Meet people		Something else	

SECTION B

1. What do you think are the <u>four</u> most important issues in Brighton today? Please put 1, 2, 3, 4 in the appropriate boxes in order of importance.

Bus Services		Civic Amenities		Environment/Architecture	
Housing		Dirty Streets & Parks		The Private Car	
Rates		Education		Social Services	
Unemployment		Property Speculation		Corrupt Councillors	

2. Here is a list of important areas of national concern. On the whole, which do you think are the <u>four</u> most important ones? Please list them in order of importance — 1, 2, 3, 4.

Defence		Industrial Relations		Foreign Policy		Education	
Housing		The Environment		Law and Order		Immigration	
Inflation		Transport		Poverty		Public Ownership	
						Unemployment	

3. Would <u>you</u> personally prefer the Labour Party to be <u>more</u> socialist, <u>less</u> socialist, or about the same?

More socialist	
Less socialist	
About the same	

4. Most people have different ideas about Socialism. Which of the list below comes closest to YOUR idea of Socialism? Please cross <u>TWO</u> only

Creating social equality		Racial Tolerance	
World peace		Abolishing social classes	
Raising the standard of living		Scientific advance	
Individual freedom		Liberating the working class	
Public ownership of production		Real democracy	
Equality of opportunity		Something else	

5. Why are there different political parties which disagree with one another? Please cross <u>ONE</u> statement only. It's because . . .

They're only in it for themselves	
They have different ideas about how to run the country best	
One represents the haves, the other the have-nots	
They're making a fuss about nothing	
Its really the working class versus the bosses	
They have different ideas about what is important	

6. Considering everything both the major political Parties stand for, would you say there is a <u>good deal</u> of difference between the Parties, <u>some</u> difference, <u>not much</u> difference, or <u>no</u> difference at all?

A good deal of difference			Not much difference	
Some difference			No difference at all	

7. Considering everything, who do you think would make the better leader of the Labour Party?

Harold Wilson		Shirley Williams		Dick Taverne	
Tony Wedgewood Benn		Dennis Healey		Edward Short	
Roy Jenkins		Jack Jones			
Michael Foot		Eric Heffer			

8. Now could you please describe in a short sentence what you would mean by 'Socialism'. In other words, "Socialism to me means . . . .

9. How would <u>you</u> describe the Labour Party? Here is a list of possible descriptions of the Labour Party. Please put a cross against the <u>one</u> which best describes the Labour Party. Put the <u>one</u> cross in the <u>right-hand</u> column. ←

	The Party of Social Reform	
	The Party of All Races	
	The Party of Ordinary People	
	The Party of Socialism	
	The Party of the Welfare State	
	The Party of the Working Class	
	The Party for World Peace	
	The Party of Technological Advance	
	The Party of All Classes	
	The Party of Democracy	

↑

10. Now in the <u>Left-hand</u> column, please put crosses alongside the <u>two</u> features of the Labour Party which you like best. Mark them 1 and 2.

SECTION C

1. Which of the following age-groups are you in?

16—24 yrs		47—52 yrs	
25—30 yrs		53—63 yrs	
31—40 yrs		64—73 yrs	
41—46 yrs		73 or more	

2. What is your current job? Can you tell me exactly what you do?

....
....
....

3. Which of the following income-groups is closest to your <u>total household</u> income?

Under £999 per year		£2000—£2999 per year		£4000—£4999 per year	
£1000—£1999 per year		£3000—£3999 per year		£5000 or more per year	

4. Are you a member of a Trade Union?   YES ☐   NO ☐
   If you are, which one(s) do you belong to? ....

5. What was or is your father's main occupation? Can you tell me exactly what he did or does?

....
....

6. Was your father a member of the Labour Party?   YES ☐   NO ☐

7. Which of the following kinds of secondary school did you go to?

Grammar School		Technical Secondary		Public School	
Secondary Modern		Comprehensive		Another type	

8. At what age did you complete your full time education?

13 yrs or under		14—15 yrs old		16—17 yrs old		18—19 yrs old		20 yrs or more	

9. People often talk about their being two main classes in Britain today, would you describe yourself as middle-class, working-class or of no particular class?

   Middle class ☐   Working class ☐   No particular class ☐

10. Which of the following activities do you regularly do in your spare time?

Listening to good music		Reading books		Do-it-yourself	
Drinking at the local		Bingo/Pools		Fishing	
Holding dinner parties		Dogs/Horses		Watching football	
Watching T.V.		Knitting		Taking-it-easy	
				Going out to dinner	

SECTION D

1. Are you currently an active member of any other political groups or campaigns? e.g. Comprehensive schools & Spa campaign, Tenant's Associations, Trade Unions, Peace campaigns, other Socialist groups, alternative newspapers, Women's Lib, Environmental and community action groups. Please list them all fully.

....

....

2. Would you say that there are more or less of these groups and campaigns now than in the past, say before 1967? | More | | Less | | Same number | |

3. Have you personally been more active or less active or just as active in these campaigns over recent years, say since 1967?

| More active | | Less active | | Just as active or Non-active | |

4. Do you yourself have any friends or relatives who are active in these groups but who are NOT members of the Labour Party? Are there . .

| Many | | Some | | One or two | | None at all | |

5. Finally, which of the following organizations in Brighton would you tend to turn to if you wanted to achieve certain things (a–i)? You may cross more than one type or organization for each issue.

	A Local Tenants' Association	An Environmental Group e.g. The Regency Society	A Left Group e.g. the International Socialists	A local Community Group	Help start a special campaign	The local Labour Party	Contact your Councillor or M.P.	The local liberal or Conservative Party	Your Trade Union or the Trades Council
a) Ban the private car from the town centre									
b) Get more council houses built									
c) Save a beautiful old building from demolition									
d) Get more nursery schools built									
e) Get property speculation stopped in Brighton									
f) Get a better Meals on Wheels service for OAPs									
g) Stop overcrowding in your kid's school									
h) Improve your local bus service									
i) Organise Brighton after the Revolution									

Thank you for your co-operation in completing this questionnaire. Please return it immediately in the stamped addressed envelope provided, or if you have lost it, send the questionnaire to 179, Lewes Road, Brighton.

in order to cover all possibilities. The results could in any case be compared with attendance records, and the categories would also allow a comparison to be made with earlier studies.

Questions 9 and 10 provided the second measure of activism, and in this I was lucky in being able to take advantage of the proximity of two rounds of local elections, which took place in the April and June prior to the survey in July–September 1973. Since local Labour parties only tend to be really active at election times, the importance of timing here was paramount. The Kemptown CLP was at a peak of mobilization at this time, so the resulting figures for activism and the total number of activists would very much represent a maximum at least for local elections.

Once again, respondents were given the opportunity first of all of saying that they had not 'done anything' in the local elections. If the list of activists had been presented first, then respondents may have been tempted either to tick-off a few activities in order to create a good impression, or to tick-off any number of activities they may have done in the past. In Question 10, where I asked respondents exactly what they had done, I provided a comprehensive list including even the minimal 'put up a window bill'. The latter is a public expression of political commitment, but is not really 'activity' in any real sense. It did, however, provide a 'let-out' for non-activists, allowing them to say that they had 'done' something. The resulting figures would seem to indicate that this technique was reasonably successful in producing accurate data.

The formulation used in Question 8 was the only feasible way of providing some indication of *past* activism in the context of this questionnaire. Officers tend to be activists in the Labour Party. 'Officer' is a fairly unambiguous term. Respondents would also be more likely to remember that they had been an officer, whereas questions about past levels of activity would be beset by memory difficulties.

Question 11 was a somewhat crude attempt to obtain data on the political motivations of Labour Party members. Possible responses, though 'forced', covered a political range from left to right and included 'social' reasons as well as a 'something else' let-out. The major aim of the question was to test the essentially sectarian commitment ('further the interests of the working class') against other possible motivations, since this was relevant to Hindess. Respondents were asked to choose only *one* main reason to force the choice between 'sectarian' and other motivations, but in fact some of the categories duplicated one another and were lumped together in the later analysis. A reasonable 'spread' of replies was also achieved.

Section B

The major concern of Section B was with the political views of Labour Party members, and questions were included on policy concerns, politics and politicians, the Labour Party, and the meaning of socialism. These for the most part were to be treated as dependent variables, which would later be correlated with independent variables such as class, age, etc.

In Questions 1 and 2 respondents were asked what *they* thought were the most important issues in Brighton and in the country as a whole. This was done in order to make comparisons with earlier data on policy concerns (e.g. Abrams and Rose), to relate these policy concerns to other variables such as activism, class and age, and to make comparisons between predominantly middle class and working class wards, such as Hindess did in Liverpool. A choice was given of 12 and 13 possible answers respectively, and respondents were asked in each question to choose four in order of importance.

In both questions, the options offered were the result of considerable deliberation. For the local issues, I sought the advice of local people including Councillors, as well as relying on my own knowledge of the town. For the national issues, I based the options offered on those used by poll firms, those used in previous research and one or two 'issues' I was particularly keen to 'test', e.g. poverty and public ownership, although I would be the first to admit that this question by no means represented a valid test of the popularity of, for instance, public ownership, given the phraseology I was forced to adopt. Nevertheless, the results would be relevant to this problem, in addition to their correlation with the variables mentioned above.

Question 3 was one of the key questions in the survey. Respondents were asked the straightforward question: 'Would *you* personally prefer the Labour Party to be *more* socialist, *less* socialist or about the same?'. The object was to provide a measure of feeling among local Labour Party members in relation to the Party's perceived stance and performance at the national level. The use of an identical phraseology also meant that comparison could be made with existing poll data on the responses of Labour *voters* and the electorate as a whole.

I was warned beforehand by one Labour Councillor that most members would feel constrained to reply 'more socialist' because nobody wanted to be in the position of saying 'less socialist', and hence appearing 'unsocialist'. This itself is not an adequate explanation because respondents could still be 'socialists' and at the same time say that they personally wanted the *Labour Party* to be *less* 'socialist' – it all depends on what each respondents' conception of 'socialism' really was. I also suspect that what he really meant was that the majority of Labour Party members would automatically say that they wanted the Party to be more 'socialist' in order to express a more general dissatisfaction with the Party. They may or may not want the Party to be more 'socialist' but more 'something'. In saying they wanted the Party to be more 'socialist', respondents could mean for instance, that they wanted less in-fighting and more principle rather than nationalization and worker's control. The answers therefore beg the question: what do members mean by 'socialist'? In an effort to find out, they were asked just that.

Question 4 was the first of these questions on the meaning of socialism. Respondents were asked which two of twelve phrases came closest to *their* idea of socialism. Once again, a wide choice of possibilities was provided, and ideas relevant to an examination of Hindess were included.

The purpose of Question 5 was to test a 'class-struggle' view of politics against two other views – the 'social democratic' and the 'cynical/apathetic'. This is surely crucial if a decline in *class* politics is proposed. The formulation of the question, 'Why are there different political parties which disagree with one another?' was meant to be thought-provoking. I saw it as an attempt to obtain some initial data on Labour Party members' perceptions of the party system. Needless to say, a simplistic forced-response question such as this has a limited value, and it is highly likely that many respondents would have liked to have put forward a more sophisticated interpretation, or to have agreed with more than one of the six statements. On the other hand, a below-average 5 per cent of the respondents refused to answer this question.

Question 6 was the standard pollster's question of the extent of the difference between the two major political parties. The intention was to correlate the replies with other variables such as class and activism. In addition, one would assume that actual members of a major political party would be *more* likely to say that there was a 'good deal' of difference between the parties. If they didn't, one would have to question why they were in the party at all.

The purpose of asking question 7 was two-fold: first, to find out what proportion of the membership would prefer a leader to the 'Left' or 'Right' of centre – as additional information on the political views of Labour Party members. Hence the choice of potential Labour Party leaders – three 'Left-wingers', three 'Right-wingers', three 'Centrists' and one Trade Union leader. Second, it was thought that such a participatory Question would be popular, and would encourage respondents to complete the full questionnaire.

Question 8 was the second of the questions on the meaning of socialism. It was open-ended and respondents were asked to complete the sentence: 'Socialism to me means . . .' Coming after the fixed-choice question on the same topic, it could be argued that respondents would be tempted to copy-out one or other of the options in the former. On the other hand, the fixed-choice did cover a wide range of the sort of answers that one would expect to be offered, and reversing the sequence may not have avoided the problem anyway. Moreover, it had to be placed in this section because it would have seemed out of place anywhere else. It also had to be placed near the end of Section B. Had such a 'difficult' question been placed higher up the order, the response-rate would have been badly affected. In the event, some 18·5 per cent of all respondents failed to complete this question, against an average non-response for the 'political' questions of 5·9 per cent. If it had been placed at the top of the page, i.e. before the fixed-choice question on socialism, it is quite possible that a similar percentage would have ignored the rest of the questions.

The final questions in this section, numbers 9 and 10, were about members' views of the Labour Party. Respondents were asked how they would best *describe* the Labour Party, and what two features they *liked* best about the Labour Party. A similar question was asked by Abrams and Rose in *Must Labour Lose?*,[1] and most of the response-categories came from that survey. The format was a little ambitious for this kind of self-completion exercise, and this affected the response-rate, particularly to Question 10 (15·3 per cent didn't answer). Nevertheless the spread of replies indicated that the options offered were valid, and that the question was on the whole understood.

Section C

The key demographic variables of age, occupation, income and education were obtained in response to the questions in Section C.

Question 1 was formulated in terms of age-groups, rather than a direct question asking the respondents to give their age. This was done in order, first, to reduce non-response, and in this it was successful – only 3 per cent refused to answer the question. Second, classification into a simple but

[1] Abrams, M., Rose, R. and Hinden, R., *Must Labour Lose?*, Penguin, 1960.

comprehensive set of eight different age-cohorts would also assist the later analysis.

For Question 2 on occupation, the familiar and tested phraseology of 'What is your current job ? Can you tell me exactly what you do?' was deemed the most satisfactory method of obtaining accurate occupational data, though some took it a little too literally, like two respondents who wrote: 'I work as an office cleaner for a solicitor. I sweep, dust, polish, scrub, hoover, wash-up etc.' and 'Universal Precision Grinder – carry out all grinding requirements for a small machine shop making industrial vibrators – also assemble and test vibrators, do some turning, milling and drilling if there is not much grinding to be done'.

Only 5 per cent refused to disclose their occupation, and of these, it was obvious that most of them were pensioners because they were mostly beyond retirement age. However, I did regret not asking those who had retired what kind of employment they had been in, and housewives what their husbands did. But I have no reason to believe that either the occupations of retired persons differed significantly from those in employment, or that the classification of non-working housewives by their husband's occupations would have affected the results to any significant extent. Needless to say, had separate questions on this topic been included, then something else would have had to be left out, if I was to keep down the length of this self-completion exercise.

Question 3 involved total household income, and here again the 'income group' formulation was used, and I considered it most appropriate to ask for total household rather than each individual member's income. This would provide useful subsidiary data on class.

Question 4 was a pretty straightforward one, merely asking respondents whether they were members of a trade union, and if so, which one. Some confusion may have resulted here in relation to those who belonged to staff associations or trade unions not affiliated to the TUC, but in practice a large number of respondents included these, though one never knows how many didn't. In the case of retired persons, some voluntarily mentioned that they had been trade union members, but they were not coded as current trade union members. Once again, it would have been useful to specifically ask retired persons about past trade union membership, but given my constraints, this was not possible.

Father's occupation was the subject of Question 5. The purpose of this was to obtain information on the class-background of current Labour Party members. Unfortunately, but not unpredictably, some 21 per cent of the respondents did not answer this question. Nevertheless, the data obtained proved useful in analysing mobility in relation to other variables. I also asked respondents in Question 6 whether their father had been a member of the Labour Party. This was included because it had been suggested from observation that membership of the party often tended to be very much a matter of family tradition.

Questions 7 and 8 were concerned with the educational background of current Labour Party members, and a comprehensive list of possibilities was included for both type of school attended and for terminal age of education. I did, however, omit to include the category of 'Elementary' in the list of types of school attended, but in practice it seemed likely that most respondents who had only attended elementary school crossed the 'another type' box, and some wrote it in. In any case, the main purpose of the question was to find out the proportion of the membership who had either been to public school, grammar school, or comprehensive school, so that they might be compared with 'the rest'.

Question 9 was a standard formulation of a 'self-assigned class' question. The phrasing adopted was reasonably 'neutral', and a 'no particular class' option was included. Only 4 per cent didn't answer this question.

Question 10 on spare-time activities, was included to be used as a subsidiary data on, or as a kind of cultural dimension of, class. The categories offered were designed to be comprehensive, yet inclusive of class-specific as well as universal activities.

Section D

Section D was something of an experiment. It represented an attempt to measure the extent of social control exercised by the Labour Party over its membership. Given that it has been argued by Hindess and others that Labour Party members (as well as traditional Labour supporters) are now turning to modes of political activity other than formal party politics, in order to satisfy their needs and political demands, I therefore wanted to use the opportunity of the questionnaire survey to examine this assertion. Of course, the questions in Section D by no means represented a definitive 'test' of the hypothesis, and given the quasi-official status of the questionnaire, the credibility of the answers given in this section must rate a lot lower than those given in response to the questions in the other sections and I have not reported extensively on this section in the text. It merely represented an attempt to obtain some preliminary data relevant to this problem. This would then have to be supplemented with, for instance, interviews or discussions with Labour and non-Labour activists, non-active members, and non-Labour, non-active socialists. Even more important, the hypothesis mentioned could perhaps best be examined by observation of the local political process in action over a period of years.

In order to obtain this preliminary data relevant to the problem of Labour's social control over its members, I decided to look at two aspects. First, participation by existing Labour Party members in other forms of political activity, and second, the extent to which Labour Party members are prepared to turn to other organizations or types of activities in order to raise issues or achieve goals.

In addition, in Questions 2 and 3 I asked members whether they con- campaigns in which they were *active* members, giving examples. Since I was concerned with non-Labour Party *activity*, I didn't ask for mere 'membership' which would have been less meaningful. For instance, quiescent membership of the Local Resident's Association would have not been relevant to the hypothesis.

In addition, in Questions 2 and 3 I asked members whether they considered that there was now more or less such groups and campaigns, and whether they personally had been more or less active in this way over recent years. Members were also asked whether they had any non-Labour Party friends or relatives who were active in these groups, and if so, how many.

Finally, in the last question, members were asked to indicate which of nine different organizations they would turn to if they wanted to achieve certain goals. I was careful to choose goals which I knew were among the most 'topical' locally. They also included those which the local Labour party was most concerned with, at least in terms of policy pronouncements, and those which one would *expect* the Labour Party to be most concerned with.

However, it was the organizations and activities which I was testing, not the issues. Unfortunately some respondents were a little confused by the complexity of this question, and assumed that it was the issues and not the organizations which were being tested. These had to be eliminated from the analysis, and as a result 18 per cent of the answers to this question were lost. In fact, this was clearly a 'difficult' section for many respondents, and an almost equally large non-response was obtained in the three previous questions, partly because it was located on a separate side of the questionnaire. On the other hand, Questions 1 and 5 yielded some useful data which could provide a basis for further investigation.

In concluding this section on questionnaire design, I would merely re-emphasize the constraints with which I was working. The questionnaire had to be concise and economic. I had no grant to support the survey. There were, of course, many questions I would have liked to ask but couldn't, and there were many problems which really needed to be explored in depth. Nor have I mentioned all the possible uses I had in mind when designing the questions.

Suffice to say that almost all the questions eventually included were 'essentials' which would prove particularly useful in testing the arguments of Hindess and others.

Finally, that a very reasonable overall response-rate was achieved by this self-completion questionnaire when so many of the sample could hardly be described as Labour Party 'members' and that non-response to each question usually amounted to only a very small percentage, is I believe, something of a vote of confidence in the design, format, and style of the questionnaire. In support of this, I would like to quote a dustman from the Whitehawk Council Estate who returned his questionnaire with a note saying: 'I would like say I enjoyed filling this form in I think we should have more of these as it makes you feel as if were part of the town and not a outcast'.

Appendix B

Percentage Turnout of Registered Electors, Municipal Elections, County Borough of Brighton 1919–1973

Year	Wards now in Kemptown Constituency	Wards now in Pavilion Constituency	Total Number of Contests	Average Turnout, County Borough of Brighton
1919	41·1	41·2	10	41·2
1920	46·2	42·7	9	45·1
1921	33·7	41·3	10	37·5
1922	35·4	38·4	8	37·3
1923	34·5	47·3	8	39·3
1924	28·6	40·4	6	34·5
1925	41·7	44·8	4	44·0
1926	37·7	45·7	11	41·4
1927	36·5	44·7	7	40·0
1928	37·2	39·9	5	38·3
1929	30·3	37·3	15	33·6
1930	35·4	34·6	9	35·0
1931	41·9	50·4	13	45·8
1932	33·3	40·7	12	36·4
1933	32·8	49·1	9	40·1
1934	36·3	43·6	11	39·6
1935	38·9	46·8	7	41·2
1936	37·5	47·8	10	41·2
1937	36·4	39·4	5	38·2
1938	38·0	42·2	13	40·0
1939–1944	No regular elections			
1945	34·5	41·8	19	38·4
1946	30·6	39·7	19	35·4
1947	45·1	44·2	16	44·7
1948	No elections			
1949	45·7	48·1	13	46·6
1950	43·4	36·1	18	39·8
1951	40·3	43·7	11	41·0
1952	50·9	43·0	14	48·1

154

Year	Wards now in Kemptown Constituency	Wards in Pavilion Constituency	Total Number of Contests	Average Turnout, County Borough of Brighton
1953	48·2	46·0	17	47·1
1954	43·8	39·1	15	41·6
1955	42·5	41·7	12	42·1
1956	42·7	44·7	7	43·6
1957	44·4	45·0	7	44·6
1958	40·0	42·4	12	41·2
1959	41·1	43·6	12	41·7
1960	36·5	34·6	13	35·8
1961	38·1	44	11	39·2
1962	35·6	39·6	13	37·2
1963	40·4	42·7	14	41·6
1964	39·6	38·5	18	39·1
1965	41·3	38·3	17	40·0
1966	41·7	33·2	18	37·9
1967	46·8	37·8	19	42·5
1968	40·3	32·8	18	36·2
1969	39·6	27·9	19	34·1
1970	42·0	30·7	18	37·0
1971	40·6	33·0	19	37·0
1972	38·7	30·7	19	34·9
1973[1]	40·3	36·6	19	38·5

[1] Average turnout in both rounds of local elections, County and District.

Percentage Turnout of Registered Electors in General Elections, County Borough of Brighton 1918–1974

Year	Percentage Turnout
1918	50·3
1922	55·4
1923	68·2
1924	55·2
1929	65·1
1931	68·3
1935	61·7
1945	64·3

	Kemptown Percentage Turnout	Pavilion Percentage Turnout
1950	78·0	78·9
1951	77·1	75·5
1955	70·0	67·5
1959	73·8	69·8
1964	72·2	70·1
1966	80·0	70·3
1970	75·1	66·6
Feb. 1974	78·7	76·1

Appendix C

Affiliated Membership of the Labour Party in Brighton.
Affiliation Fees Paid to Party Headquarters. 1911–1973[1]

Year	Organization	Members	Fees
1911	Brighton Labour Representation Committee	—	15s
1912–15	—	—	—
1916	Trades Council	—	15s
1917	—	—	—
1918	Brighton and Hove Labour Party	—	£1 10s
1919	Brighton and Hove Labour Party	—	£1 10s
1920	Brighton and Hove Labour Party	—	£2 10s
1921	—	—	—
1922	Brighton and Hove Labour Party	—	£3 0s
1923	—	—	—
1924	Brighton and Hove Labour Party	—	£3 0s
1925	Brighton and Hove Labour Party	—	£3 0s
1926	Brighton and Hove Labour Party	—	£3 0s
1927	Brighton and Hove Labour Party	—	£3 0s
1928	Brighton and Hove Trades Council and Labour Party	—	£3 0s
1929	Brighton and Hove Trades Council and Labour Party	200	£3 0s
1930	Brighton and Hove Trades Council and Labour Party	414	£6 0s
1931	Brighton and Hove Trades Council and Labour Party	480	£6 0s
1932	Brighton and Hove Trades Council and Labour Party	480	£8 0s
1933	Brighton and Hove Labour Party	480	£8 0s
1934	Brighton and Hove Labour Party	480	£8 0s
1935	Brighton and Hove District Labour Party	595	£10 0s
1936	Brighton and Hove District Labour Party	762	£13 0s
1937	—	—	—
1938	Brighton and Hove Trades Council and Labour Party	2505	£47 0s
1939	Brighton and Hove Labour Party	559	£10 0s
1940	Brighton and Hove Labour Party	559	£10 0s

[1] Source: Labour Party Annual Reports.

Year	Organization		Members	Fees
1941	Brighton and Hove Labour Party		535	£10 0s
1942	Brighton and Hove Labour Party		480	£10 0s
1943	Brighton and Hove Labour Party		480	£10 0s
1944	Brighton and Hove Labour Party		480	£10 0s
1945	Brighton and Hove Labour Party		780	£16 0s
1946	Brighton and Hove Labour Party		1305	£27 0s
1947	Brighton and Hove Labour Party		1423	£30 0s
1948	—		—	—
1949	Kemptown Labour Party	975	Pavilion Labour Party	491
1950	Kemptown Labour Party	1786	Pavilion Labour Party	681
1951	Kemptown Labour Party	2224	Pavilion Labour Party	693
1952	Kemptown Labour Party	2532	Pavilion Labour Party	935
1953	Kemptown Labour Party	2279	Pavilion Labour Party	1056
1954	Kemptown Labour Party	—	Pavilion Labour Party	—
1955	Kemptown Labour Party	1652	Pavilion Labour Party	823
1956	Kemptown Labour Party	—	Pavilion Labour Party	—
1957	Kemptown Labour Party	— (1107)[1]	Pavilion Labour Party	—
1958	Kemptown Labour Party	—	Pavilion Labour Party	—
1959	Kemptown Labour Party	— (919)	Pavilion Labour Party	—
1960	Kemptown Labour Party	1043 (730)	Pavilion Labour Party	800
1961	Kemptown Labour Party	1006 (640)	Pavilion Labour Party	800
1962	Kemptown Labour Party	— (800)	Pavilion Labour Party	—
1963	Kemptown Labour Party	— (924)	Pavilion Labour Party	1000
1964	Kemptown Labour Party	1135 (1053)	Pavilion Labour Party	1000
1965	Kemptown Labour Party	1471 (1232)	Pavilion Labour Party	1000
1966	Kemptown Labour Party	— (1141)	Pavilion Labour Party	1000
1967	Kemptown Labour Party	1316 (1112)	Pavilion Labour Party	1000
1968	Kemptown Labour Party	1093 (843)	Pavilion Labour Party	1000
1969	Kemptown Labour Party	1000 (628)	Pavilion Labour Party	1000
1970	Kemptown Labour Party	1000 (814)	Pavilion Labour Party	1000
1971	Kemptown Labour Party	1000 (880)	Pavilion Labour Party	1000
1972	Kemptown Labour Party	1000 (910)	Pavilion Labour Party	1000
1973	Kemptown Labour Party	1000 (927)	Pavilion Labour Party	1000 (384)

[1] Figures in Brackets from Local Party Annual Reports and Records.

Selected Bibliography

Abrams, Mark, Rose, Richard and Hinden, Rita, *Must Labour Lose?* Penguin, 1960.

Attlee, C. R., *The Labour Party in Perspective*. Gollancz, 1937.

Anderson, Perry and Blackburn, Robin (eds.), *Towards Socialism*. Fontana, 1965.

Barker, Bernard (Ed. and Intro. by), *Ramsay MacDonald's Political Writings*. Allen Lane, 1972.

Barratt Brown, Michael, *From Labourism to Socialism*, The Political Economy of Labour in the 1970s. Spokesman, 1972.

Baxter, R., 'The Working Class and Labour Politics'. *Political Studies*, Vol. XX, No. 1, 1972, pp. 97–107.

Bealey, Frank (Ed. and Intro. by), *The Social and Political Thought of the British Labour Party*. Weidenfeld and Nicolson, 1970.

Bealey, Frank and Pelling, Henry, *Labour and Politics 1900–1906*. A History of The Labour Representation Committee. Macmillan, 1958.

Bealey, Frank, Blondel, J., and McCann, W. P., *Constituency Politics – A Study of Newcastle-Under-Lyme*. Faber and Faber, 1965.

Beattie, Alan (Ed.), *English Party Politics Vol II: The Twentieth Century*. Weidenfeld and Nicolson, 1970.

Beer, Samuel H., *Modern British Politics*. A Study of Parties and Pressure Groups. Faber, 2nd edn., 1969.

Benney, Mark, Gray, A. P., and Pear, R. H., *How People Vote*. A study of Electoral Behaviour in Greenwich. Routledge, 1956.

Berry, David. *The Sociology of Grass Roots Politics*. A Study of Party Membership. Macmillan, 1970.

Birch, A. H. *Small Town Politics*. A Study of Political Life in Glossop. Oxford, 1959.

Blondel, J. *Voters, Parties and Leaders*. The Social Fabric of British Politics. Pelican, 1963, new edn. 1974.

Blondel, J. 'The Conservative Association and the Labour Party in Reading'. *Political Studies*, Vol. VI, No. 2. (1958), pp. 101–119.

Bonham, John. *The Middle Class Vote*. Faber and Faber, 1954.

Brennan, T., Cooney, E. W., and Pollins, H. *Social Change in South West Wales*. Watts, 1954.

Burgess, Tyrell, *et al. Matters of Principle – Labour's Last Chance*. Penguin, 1968.

Butler, David and Pinto-Duschinsky, Michael. *The British General Election of 1970*. Macmillan, 1971.

Butler, David and Stokes, Donald. *Political Change in Britain*. Forces Shaping Electoral Choice. Pelican, 1971.

Chamberlain, Chris. 'The Growth of Support for the Labour Party in Britain'. *British Journal of Sociology*, Vol. XXIV, No. 4, Dec. 1973.

Cline, C. A., *Recruits to Labour: The British Labour Party 1914–31*. Syracuse, New York, 1963.

Coates, Ken. *The Crisis of British Socialism* – Essays on the Rise of Harold Wilson and the Fall of the Labour Party. Spokesman, 1971.

Cole, G. D. H., *et al. Socialism The British Way*. Essential Books, London, 1948.

Crosland, C. A. R. *The Future of Socialism*. Cape, 1956.

Crouch, Colin. Politics in a Technological Society. Young Fabian Pamphlet 23, Fabian Society, London, 1970.

Desmond, Shaw. *Labour – The Giant with the Feet of Clay*. Collins, 1921.

Donnison, D. V. and Plowman, D. E. G. 'The Functions of Local Labour Parties: Experiments in Research Methods'. *Political Studies*, Vol. II, 1954, pp. 154–167.

Dowse, Robert E. and Hughes, John A. *Political Sociology*. Wiley, London, 1972.

Durbin, E. F. M. *The Politics of Democratic Socialism*. An Essay on Social Policy, Routledge, 1940.

Duverger, Maurice. *The Study of Politics*. Nelson, 1972.

Duverger, Maurice. *Political Parties*. Their Organisation and Activity in the Modern State. Methuen, 3rd edn., 1964.

Epstein, Leon D. 'Socialism and the British Labour Party'. *Political Science Quarterly*, Vol. LXVI, No. 4, Dec. 1951, pp. 556–575.

Fienburgh, Wilfred, M.P. and the Manchester Fabian Society. 'Put Policy on the Agenda' – A Study of Labour Party Organization. *Fabian Journal*, No. 6, February 1952.

Fienburgh, Wilfred, M.P. 'The Future of Labour's Organization: A Comment on the Wilson Report'. *Fabian Journal*, No. 17, November 1955.

Finer, S. E. *Comparative Government*. Pelican, 1974.

Goldthorpe, John H., Lockwood, David, Bechhofer, Frank, and Platt, Jennifer. *The Affluent Worker (2): Political Attitudes and Behaviour*. Cambridge, 1968.

Gould, Julius C. 'Riverside': A Labour Constituency. A Survey of a Political Party'. *Fabian Journal*, No. 14, November 1954.

Guttsman, W. L. *The British Political Elite*. MacGibbon and Kee, 1963.

Hamilton, Mary Agnes. *The Labour Party To-Day. What it is and How it Works*. Labour Book Service, 1939.

Hampton, William. *Democracy and Community*. A Study of Politics in Sheffield, O.U.P., London, 1970.

Hindess, Barry. *The Decline of Working Class Politics*. MacGibbon and Kee, 1971.

Janosik, Edward G. *Constituency Labour Parties in Britain*. Pall Mall, 1968.

Jenkins, Roy. *What Matters Now*. Fontana, 1972.

Jones, G. W. *Borough Politics. A Study of the Wolverhampton Town Council, 1888–1964*. Macmillan, 1969.

Lapping, Brian. *The Labour Government 1964–70*. Penguin, 1970.

Lichtheim, George. *A Short History of Socialism*. Weidenfeld and Nicolson, 1970.

Licinius. *Vote Labour? Why?* Gollancz, 1945.

Lipset, Seymour Martin. *Political Man*. Heinemann, 1960.

Mann, Michael. *Consciousness and Action Among the Western Working Class*. Macmillan, 1973.

McHenry, Dean E. *The Labour Party in Transition 1931–38*. Routledge, 1938.

McKenzie, R. T. *British Political Parties*. The Distribution of Power Within the Conservative and Labour Parties. Heinemann, 2nd edn., 1963.

McKenzie, R. T., 'Labour Party Organization: A Note on Its Future'. *Fabian Journal*, No. 16, July 1955.

McKenzie, R. T. and Silver, A. *Angels in Marble*. Heinemann, 1968.

McKibbin, R. I. *The Evolution of the Labour Party, 1910–24*. Oxford, 1975.

Miliband, Ralph. *Parliamentary Socialism: A Study in the Politics of Labour*. Merlin Press, 1972.

Miliband, Ralph. 'Socialism and the Myth of the Golden Past', in *Socialist Register 1964*. Merlin Press, 1964, pp. 92–103.

Miliband, Ralph. *The State in Capitalist Society*. Weidenfeld and

Nicolson, 1969.

Miliband, Ralph. 'The Labour Government and Beyond', in *Socialist Register, 1966*. Merlin Press, 1966, pp. 11–25.

Milne, R. S. and MacKenzie, H. C. *Marginal Seat, 1955*. Hansard Society, 1958.

Morrison, Herbert. *The Peaceful Revolution*. Speeches by the Rt. Hon. Herbert Morrison. Allen and Unwin, 1949.

Nordlinger, Eric A. *The Working Class Tories*. MacGibbon and Kee, 1967.

Northcott, Jim. *Why Labour?* Penguin, 1964.

Panitch, Leo V. 'Ideology and Integration: The Case of the British Labour Party'. *Political Studies*, June 1971, Vol. XIX, No. 2.

Parker, John. *Labour Marches On*. Penguin, 1947.

Parkin, Frank. *Class Inequality and Political Order*. Paladin, 1972.

Pelling, H. *The Origins of the Labour Party*. Oxford, 1965.

Pelling, H. *A Short History of the Labour Party*. Macmillan, 4th edn., 1972.

Poirier, P. P. *The Advent of the Labour Party*. Allen and Unwin, 1958.

Pulzer, Peter G. J. *Political Representation and Elections in Britain*. Allen and Unwin, 1967.

Rawson, D. W. 'The Life-Span of Labour Parties'. *Political Studies,* Vol. XVII, No. 3, (1969), pp. 313–33.

Roberts, Robert. *The Classic Slum – Salford Life in the First Quarter of the Century*. Pelican, 1973.

Rose, Richard (Ed.). *Studies in British Politics*. A Reader in Political Sociology. Macmillan, 2nd edn., 1969.

Runciman, W. G. *Relative Deprivation and Social Justice*. Routledge, 1966.

Rush, Michael and Althoff, Philip. *An Introduction to Political Sociology*. Nelson, 1971.

Saville, John. 'Labourism and the Labour Government', in *Socialist Register 1967*. Merlin Press, 1967, pp. 43–71.

Scanlon, John. *The Decline and Fall of the Labour Party*. Preface by James Maxton, Davies, 1932.

Seabrook, Jeremy. *The Unpriviledged*. A Hundred Years of Family Life and Tradition in a Working-Class Street. Penguin, 1973.

Seyd, Patrick. *Bulletin of the Society for the Study of Labour History*. No. 24, Spring 1972, pp. 82–85. Review of Hindess.

Sharpe, L. J. *A Metropolis Votes*. London School of Economics, 1962.

S.S.R.C. Proceedings of the Social Science Research Council Conference on '*The Occupational Community of the Traditional Worker*'. Durham, 1973.

Wertheimer, Egon. *Portrait of the Labour Party*. Putnam, 1929.

Westergaard, J. H. 'Sociology: The Myth of Classlessness', in *Ideology in Social Science*, ed. Robin Blackburn, Fontana, 1972.

Williams, Francis. *Fifty Years' March — The Rise of the Labour Party*. Odhams, 1950.

Williams, Raymond (Ed.). *May Day Manifesto 1968*. Penguin, 1968.

Index

163

N. 6